Remembering
Camden

D0891115

REMEMBERING
Camden

STORIES FROM AN OLD MAINE HARBOR

BARBARA F. DYER

Charleston London

History
PRESS

Published by The History Press
Charleston, SC 29403
www.historypress.net

Copyright © 2007 by Barbara F. Dyer
All rights reserved

All images courtesy of Camden Area History Center, from Barbara F. Dyer Collection, unless otherwise noted.

First published 2007

Manufactured in the United Kingdom

ISBN 978.1.59629.321.2

Library of Congress Cataloging-in-Publication Data

Dyer, Barbara F.
Remembering Camden : stories from an old Maine harbor / Barbara F. Dyer.
p. cm.
ISBN 978-1-59629-321-2 (alk. paper)
1. Camden (Me. : Town)--History--20th century--Anecdotes. 2. Camden (Me.
: Town)--Social life and customs--20th century--Anecdotes. 3. Camden (Me. :
Town)--Biography--Anecdotes. 4. Camden Region (Me.)--History,
Local--Anecdotes. I. Title.
F29.C2D938 2007
974.1'53--dc22
                          2007041971

Notice: The information in this book is true and complete to the best of our knowledge. It is offered without guarantee on the part of the author or The History Press. The author and The History Press disclaim all liability in connection with the use of this book.

All rights reserved. No part of this book may be reproduced or transmitted in any form whatsoever without prior written permission from the publisher except in the case of brief quotations embodied in critical articles and reviews.

Contents

CONTENTS

Camden's Birth Certificate

Next May, it will have been 239 years since Camden's first settler, James Richards, sailed into Camden Harbor. He was followed by Major William Minot and Lewis Ogier. Then Robert Thorndike came the same year to Goose River with his brother, Paul Thorndike, and James Simonton. Then to Clam Cove came William Gregory, William Porter and William Upham.

By the time 331 people had settled in Camden, they felt it should have a town government. So on February 17, 1791, the plantation of Cambden became incorporated as the seventy-second town in the state. It had three readings in the House of Representatives, passed and signed by David Cobb, Speaker. Then it had two readings in the Senate, passed and signed by Samuel Phillips, president. It was approved by none other than John Hancock, who was governor of Massachusetts at that time. All three signers were leaders in the Revolutionary War.

The document read:

COMMONWEALTH OF MASSACHUSETTS

In the year of our Lord, one thousand seven hundred and ninety-one. An act to incorporate the Plantation of Cambden, in the county of Hancock into a town by the name of Cambden.

Be it enacted by the Senate and House of Representatives in the General Court assembled and by authority of the same, that the said Plantation called Cambden, included within the following boundaries, viz: Beginning at a rock marked A.X. on the seashore at the north side of Owl's Head Bay at the southeast corner of Thomaston line; thence running northwest by north, seven miles, thirty-four poles, to a maple stake marked on four sides, and a pile of stones; thence running northeast, five miles, ninety-four poles, to a beech tree marked on four sides; thence running east three miles and one half and twenty poles, to a spruce tree marked on four sides; thence running south east by south, one mile to a fir tree marked on four sides at Little Ducktrap, in Penobscot Bay; thence by the sea shore in a westerly direction to the bounds first mentioned; together with the inhabitants thereon, be and they hereby are incorporated into a Town by the name of Cambden; and that the said Town be and hereby is, vested with all the Powers, Privileges and Immunities which other Towns in this Commonwealth may by law enjoy.

And be it enacted further by the authority aforesaid, that Oliver Parker, Esq.. of Penobscot be and hereby is empowered to issue his warrant, directed to some principal Inhabitant of said Town of Cambden, requiring him to notify the Inhabitants there of to meet at such a time and place as he shall therein appoint, to choose such Officers as Towns are by law required to choose at their annual meeting in the month of March or April.

Camden had been named for Lord Camden, who had been kind to the colonists, and the "b" in the spelling is believed to have been a mistake that was corrected in 1805.

In 1794, the commonwealth of Massachusetts had a law that any town would be fined for not having a gospel minister. Previous to that time there was very little preaching in Camden, except occasionally when a "religious teacher" would stop while passing through. Upon the speaker's arrival, news would spread and a large congregation would gather for the privilege of hearing a sermon. There were about three ordained ministers within a hundred-mile radius.

Camden "voted that David Blodgett and Sam'l Mclaughlin be the committee to draw up a petition to lay before the Supreme Court to be holden at Hallowell, against paying a fine for not having a minister for three years past."

However, the decision the committee handed down forced Camden to pay in full two pounds, fourteen shillings and six pence. After that, at town meeting, among other interesting articles, they voted to raise thirty or more pounds for support of the gospel.

Reverend Paul Coffin (believed to have been a Congregationalist) kept a journal, and wrote about his wonderful visit to Camden, where he stayed with Captain William McGlathery. He wrote about the fifteen neat houses and other buildings, making it a compact village. Today we might doubt the good minister's description of "compact." Fifteen houses in Camden— which also included Goose River (Rockport), Clam Cove (Glen Cove), West

Camden (West Rockport) and Rockville—couldn't be considered compact today. Also the harbor was full of pleasant islands. The entry had been dated August 15, 1796.

The next year every citizen was required by the commonwealth law to pay a tax for support of a religious order. In desperation perhaps, some individuals from Camden built a meetinghouse a half mile from the J.C. Curtis store on the "old post road." Today that location would have been on the northeast corner of Elm and Park Streets, across the road from Bank North, formerly known as Peoples Heritage Bank.

This is the first meetinghouse built in Camden.

A True Love Story

While studying the genealogy of the Hosmer family from 1635 to 1925, I found that it also included a touching love story. It had been written by the pseudonym of "Frank," with fictitious names for the people involved. Mary Gibbs Hosmer, granddaughter of Nathaniel Hosmer, recorded the tale when she was about eighteen years old, and it was published in the *Camden Advertiser* in 1846.

This is a true story, in my words. The Twenty Associates granted to Charles Barrett land in Hope and Appleton in hopes he could entice people to settle the land. Nathaniel Hosmer accepted and built a log cabin so he could farm near what is now Hosmer's Pond. (Fifty years ago it was Hosmer Lake.)

Nathaniel Hosmer came from Mason, New Hampshire. He went home the next winter and when he came to Camden again in the spring, he brought his sister and Job Hodgman. They married and took a farm nearby.

That summer Hosmer built a frame house and returned home to bring a lady to be his wife. She wanted very much to leave with him, but Mary Wheeler lived with a stepfather, David Blodgett. She also had a very determined mother, who had picked out a husband for her daughter: the son of a wealthy neighbor. Her mother had a difficult life, because of England and the Indians. Nothing would do except her daughter must marry someone who could give her an easy life.

Her mother had nothing against young Hosmer except he was poor, and if Mary went to live in Maine she would have to work hard for the rest of her life. Her daughter answered that she would rather have a home in the wilderness and work with a man she loved, than to live around there with a man she did not care for.

Nathaniel Hosmer settled by this pond, so it is known as Hosmer's Pond.

Nathaniel tried to see Mary, even though he was about twenty miles from her. But her mother would not let her out of the house unless she was with her. Before he left, he was able to get word to his love, through a mutual friend, that he had to meet her once more. They discussed the obstacles (mainly her mother and that woman's determination for her daughter to marry wealthy). She promised to become his bride as soon as he could get a house built on his lot in Camden.

Mrs. Blodgett heard of their secret meeting and decided her daughter should marry George by spring; therefore, Mary must receive the attentions of George now. But Mary insisted that she did not love him and would not see him. Feeling sacrificed by her mother, she told her to do anything she pleased. So the intentions were published.

Mary had a raging fever, and for three months it was a life or death situation. So now she was an ill girl. Nathaniel came in the spring to take Mary for his bride. His mother had told him what had happened. In order to get out of the house that night, she removed the shoe buckles he had given her, so mother knew it must be over between them and she had won, by keeping them separate.

After dinner Mary went to call on a friend, and told that friend of their plans. Later she could tell Mrs. Blodgett what she saw. Hosmer came in the night on horseback and picked Mary up and they came to Camden before Mrs. Blodgett could recover from the act of a disobedient child.

The happy couple was forgiven by Mary's parents. In fact, they were forgiven so much that the Blodgetts sold their New Hampshire property, came to Camden and settled near their daughter. Nathaniel's parents moved to Camden also. They lived happily as possible ever after.

A Welcoming Arch

A family member asked me last week, "Who put the arch on Union Street and why?" This relative had driven through the arch hundreds of times and wondered about it. Well, that was the easiest question thrown at me in weeks.

In an issue of the *Camden Herald* from July 26, 1926, we read:

A Practical Demonstration
That Our Latchstring Is Out

Camden's New Welcoming Arch
on Union Street—A Thing of
Beauty—Has Made Hit With
Visiting Tourists.

It is a known fact that hundreds of motoring tourists, in the course of a day's run, go through many towns and villages without ever knowing the name of the place they are entering. Feeling that Camden, "The Prettiest Spot in Maine," nestled at the foot of Camden Hills on the shore of the beautiful Penobscot, should not be passed by, the energetic Camden Board of Trade raised the necessary means to erect the welcoming arch.

The arch is a thing of beauty, simple and chaste in its design, being solid concrete and painted pure white. It is unlike most arches of similar character, in that it is not plastered with a hideous multitude of inscriptions by which it is endeavored to display the town's history. The only letters upon this arch are two simple inscriptions across the top of each side, reading "Entering Camden" and "Leaving Camden." This lettering is done with pure gold leaf, making a most pleasing appearance to the eye.

Camden's archway on Union Street is a Camden landmark.

The dimensions of the new arch are fourteen feet, two inches in height, and twenty-two feet in width. The columns are five feet square at the base and taper to three and a half feet at the top. At night, the cross section is outlined in electric lights, making a striking appearance. The idea of having such an arch erected was that of George E. Allen, and as a result of his energetic effort, the board of trade was induced to father the proposition. The structure was designed by Adin Hopkins and the contract for the erection was awarded to Kendall Hopkins, contractor and builder of Camden.

There are two things to know of days gone by. One is that the board of trade handled many things before Camden had a chamber of commerce. The second thing is that Union Street was the main route through town, before Elm Street became Route 1.

In the famous Camden-made movie *Peyton Place* of 1957, it shows the actor Lee Philips driving through this arch as the movie begins. Of course, the inscription "Entering Camden" had to be changed to "Entering Peyton Place."

On December 13, 1984, Camden residents were shocked to learn that the arch that had spanned Union Street for over fifty years had been demolished. This so-called divider between Camden and Rockport, was no more. It seems that a flatbed pulp truck going under just happened to be six inches too high to clear the structure.

A Welcoming Arch

Although Union Street had not been the main route for years, many people did not want to see the landmark gone. The Camden Women's Club took on the project. The group raised money in various ways, and gratefully accepted donations to erect another arch.

A replica went up in July of 1985 (a few feet higher, just in case). It reads "Welcome to Camden" on one side and "Welcome to Rockport" on the other side. Also there is a bronze plaque that proclaims the replacement by the Camden Women's Club under its president, Kay Warren. Greene Construction repaired the arch, based on Chris Fasoldt's design.

With many thanks to all, we have a welcoming arch once again; but like people and everything else, it is showing its age. In fact, it needed a major face-lift, and the department of transportation might enter into the picture to aid in this reconstruction. The town of Camden voted to donate $10,000 to the project, and the local Rotary Clubs did take it on as a project. It is once again a thing of beauty and is very well done.

After all, it is a landmark.

Catching a Rumrunner

Did you ever catch a rumrunner? Maybe you are just not ancient enough. But I'd better begin by giving you a little background.

Camden had entered the temperance movement before Neal Dow, whom they called America's father of Prohibition, had enacted the Maine Law. He worked in his father's tannery business, and when he had any free time he went around Portland, Maine, trying to do away with the evils of alcohol. Nearly all workmen had their break by drinking grog (rum and blackstrap molasses). In Camden, Deacon Joseph Stetson converted his shipyard workers to drinking coffee, even before Prohibition. He bought two large coffeepots, and the surviving one is called "the Old General."

Most churches in town had a Temperance Pledge that the members signed. The "Lincoln-Lee" Pledge read as follows: "Whereas the use of intoxicating liquors as a beverage is productive in pauperism, degradation and crime and believing it is our duty to discourage that which produces more evil than good, we therefore pledge ourselves to abstain from the use of intoxicating liquors as a beverage."

Neal Dow worked hard and long on the issue. In 1846, he won the law of Prohibition from the legislature. While he was mayor of Portland, he had been able to get Prohibition forces across the state of Maine, and the Maine Law went into effect in 1858. That marked the beginning of Prohibition (and the end of Neal Dow's popularity). Part of that law stated that liquor could only be used for medicinal purposes. I understand that many Camden men seemed to be ill during that time.

Between 1924 and 1933, over two hundred United States Coast Guard patrol vessels had been built to patrol against illegal shipments of liquor. They cost about $35,000 each and had one-pounder deck guns, plus a pair of light machine guns aboard each vessel.

"The Old General" coffeepot was used for the beginning of coffee breaks.

Other United States Coast Guard vessels, like the 159-foot *Kickapoo*, were used not only for chasing down illegal liquor, but also occasionally to find other smuggled items such as fish, furs and cattle.

The deal, to make big money, went like this. A rumrunner would purchase two-gallon cans of Belgian grain alcohol from Newfoundland, bring them into our rockbound coasts in Maine and take it by truck to Boston. The difficulty was that the rumrunners had high-speed powerboats that picked up their illegal goods from the large vessels just off the twelve-mile limit and brought them to shore. Vessels like the *Kickapoo* really were icebreakers, and only did ten to twelve knots per hour.

Most of the people in Maine wanted alcohol. Many of the men in Camden made home-brew that they kept behind the kitchen stove until it was ready. I do remember that it had yeast, malt and a few other ingredients in it. Then they bottled it right at home with a little gadget that put the caps on the bottles. But they preferred real alcohol.

During the Depression, money and jobs were scarce. One might earn ten dollars for a quick trip smuggling liquor, so some good people did get involved in the business. Well, I got involved, as a child of only seven years old. I may have been the youngest Carry Nation (Carry Amelia Moore Nation) on record. Although she died before I was born, they called her a fanatic believer in the temperance movement. She went to large cities and attacked saloons with her hatchet. But I am not violent.

My brother and I used to go down to the end of our street to play on the shore. The so-called "summer-people" lived in cottages on the shore and left for their city homes by September. We had to find our own entertainment during the Depression.

We would hear a speedboat coming toward the shore, and we would quickly hide. There were many cottages where the rumrunners could hide the liquor under the porches, and no one was around to see them (or so they thought). As soon as we would hear them speed away, we would find the cans of liquor, empty them on the ground and run for home.

We found that very exciting, but wondered how the bootleggers felt when they came to find only empty cans. Maybe the coast guard vessels were too slow, but we helped them out. Luckily we never got caught, by the rumrunners, the bootleggers or our mother.

"Remember the *Maine*—
To Hell with Spain"

None of you readers remember the Spanish-American War. Maybe some of you even wonder why the battleship *Maine*, which was blown up in Havana, Cuba's harbor, was the prelude to that war. We had Camden men in that war, so here is the story.

President McKinley dispatched the impressive battleship USS *Maine* from Key West to Havana, arriving on January 25, 1898. It measured 319 feet in length and displaced 6,682 tons, making it the largest ship ever to enter the harbor. It may have been called second class to some, as it already was nine years old. But it was unique, being one of our country's first steel warships, designed and built by Americans and the largest one ever constructed by a United States Navy yard. Although it had four ten-inch breech-loading rifles and other smaller armaments, it had been painted white, like all our vessels in peacetime.

Most of Captain Sigsbee's 24 naval officers graduated from Annapolis, but 20 percent of the 290 sailors were foreign-born American immigrants. Also aboard they had a 40-man marine guard, commanded by Lieutenant Catlin.

Their mission was to be a peaceful one, even though there was the potential that the unrest in Cuba might turn violent. The captain told his crew that there would be no shore leaves in Cuba; they could just bask in the tropical sun of the Caribbean. After a short stay, they looked forward to arriving at New Orleans just in time for Mardi Gras.

The Spanish welcomed the sailors by sending a case of sherry to the officers' mess, along with an invitation to a bullfight. Captain Sigsbee and a few of his officers accepted the invitation, but went in civilian clothes. While they were there, someone handed the captain an anti-American propaganda pamphlet with a message scrawled across it reading, "Watch out for your ship."

The men were now on the alert. By February 15, nothing had happened and they were bored. So that night the captain began a letter to his family, while marine fifer Newton played "Taps" to end the day.

The Captain's letter read, "I laid down my pen to listen to the notes of the bugle, which were singularly beautiful in the oppressive stillness of the night. The Marine bugler, Newton, who was rather given fanciful effects, was doing his best. During his pauses the echoes floated back to the ship."

At 9:10 p.m., Newton sounded the last note and returned below deck. Little did he realize that he had played his own eulogy.

Later the captain testified, "I was enclosing my letter in its envelope when the explosion came. It was a bursting, rending, and crashing roar of immense volume, largely metallic in character. It was followed by heavy, ominous metallic sounds. There was a trembling and lurching motion of the vessel, a list to port. The electric lights went out. There was intense blackness and smoke."

The situation could not be mistaken. The *Maine* had been blown up and was sinking. Lieutenant Catlin testified that he heard a sound like the crack of a pistol, followed by second roar that engulfed the ship's entire forward section. That section of the *Maine* had broken in half.

The remains of the USS *Maine* showed only a small pile of twisted metal, and the mast still displayed the colors. Of the 26 officers, 2 went down with the battleship, along with 222 sailors and 28 marines. Of the survivors, 59 were wounded and 8 were so badly hurt that they died as a result of their wounds.

Everyone in the United States wondered why the ship had exploded, and later they believed it was the enemy that caused it.

President McKinley did not want to see another war; Theodore Roosevelt did. But a war could not be avoided. McKinley sent his final terms to Spain: declare an armistice; end the reconcentration policy in Cuba and begin the process of granting Cuba independence.

On April 25, 1898, a war waiting to happen became official. To put it briefly, this war between Spain and the United States resulted, in which Spain ceded Puerto Rico, the Philippine Islands and Guam to the United States and abandoned all claims to Cuba, which became independent in 1902.

In May of 1938, a bronze tablet fixed to a boulder was placed in Harbor Park in Camden, Maine, to honor the local Spanish War soldiers. It reads:

IN MEMORIAM, LEST WE FORGET, THE MEN WHO VOLUNTEERED THEIR SERVICES TO THE CASE OF LIBERTY IN THE WAR WITH SPAIN THAT A NATION MIGHT ENJOY PEACE AND PROSPERITY THE BIRTHRIGHT OF ALL MEN.

ERECTED BY FREEMAN HERRICK CAMP NO. 18.U.S.W.V. AUXILIARY
AND FRIENDS
1938.

On one side of the boulder is the inscription. On the other side are listed the names of the men who served: John Bird, Edwin G. Bennett, Charles A. Churchill, Carl F. Cole, Alfred L. McIntyre, Gorham J. Dean, Edward Diplock, Walter E. Higgins, George W. Higgins, Allie O. Pillsbury, Ralph W. Richards, Amos D. Stockwell, Fred O. Wooster, Joshua G. Wentworth. Lyford L. Mills, Albert Feltham, Horace A. Gerald, Fred R. Rice, Frank W. Trull, Joseph A. Phelps, Charles C. Cameron, Ralph L. Higgins, Charles P. Freeman, Herbert E. Payson, William A. Herrick and Bert R. McInyre.

A boulder was placed in Harbor Park in honor of the Camden men in the Spanish-American War.

Typhoid Mary

Some of you may be too young to have heard the expression "Typhoid Mary," which refers to anyone who carried the germ and spread it to others, although "Mary" did not have the disease herself. Actually a "Typhoid Mary" did exist, and she came to Islesboro, Maine.

To begin with, typhoid fever is one of the most contagious communicable diseases, and it kills. At the turn of the last century, many people died from it. Statistics show that in 1906, about twenty-five thousand people died in our country from this dreaded disease. Symptoms include a very high fever, nausea, diarrhea, nosebleeds and a rose-colored rash.

An attractive, young Irish lady named Mary Mallon excelled in cooking. She obtained cooking jobs for some very wealthy families with no trouble. For a long time, no one knew for a long time that she was a typhoid carrier. The deadly bacilli found a happy environment in her body. Billions of germs hatched daily in her gallbladder, making her the first identified carrier of the disease in America.

The search for the carrier began on August 27, 1906, when the daughter of New York banker Charles Warren became very ill at the family's summer home in Oyster Bay, New York. It did not alarm them at first. But when the girl began to have all the symptoms of typhoid fever, they rushed her to a hospital, where she died soon after admission. Five more people in the same household soon became seriously ill, and another died.

Experts had always believed typhoid to be a disease of dirt. They thought that it probably resulted by eating shellfish from polluted waters, or possibly it came from drinking contaminated water or milk. Perhaps it came from eating food that was spoiled. After checking out all of these believed causes, the source of illness in the Warren home remained a mystery. The owner of the home, compelled to find the cause, hired investigator Soper, a sanitary

Anne Kilham painted a picture of Grindle Point Light at the entrance of Islesboro. *Courtesy of the artist Anne Kilham.*

engineer in the Department of Health in New York City. Soper eliminated all the possible sources.

A German bacteriologist named Koch had recently developed a new theory that a person could be immune to the germ, and yet have the bacteria present in his or her body, thus spreading the disease. Mr. Soper began to use that approach in his investigation.

The history of each person in the household seemed to be quite usual, but the cook had disappeared without telling anyone soon after the sickness began in the Warren household. Unfortunately, she was a walking killer.

As Mr. Soper's investigation carried on, he found seven homes in a ten-year period where twenty-eight people had typhoid. Mary had been at all of those homes. Next she started an epidemic in Ithaca, New York, where she cooked for a banker. The total cases in Ithica numbered thirteen hundred victims.

Mr. Soper got lucky one day in 1907. He heard about a Park Avenue mansion where many people were ill from typhoid. Rushing there, he asked to see Mary Mallon. They had no one there by that name, but the cook fit her description: about forty years old, light hair, blue eyes, a sharp nose and buxom figure.

Mr. Soper tried to reason with her, telling her that he needed a sample of her blood or urine. Mallon became so frightened that she grabbed a large carving knife; Mr. Soper left. He ordered his men to follow her, because the only way he could prove his case was to get her to a hospital for tests. The desperate woman clawed and bit those who came near her, but finally lost the battle. Tests taken proved that she was a typhoid carrier.

The doctors strongly suggested that Mallon have her gallbladder removed, as that would probably end the problem. She felt they really wanted to murder her, so she refused to have the operation. They kept her under constant guard, and of course she was not allowed to handle food.

The health department later formed a new policy on carriers, stating that there was to be no more isolation. Before he set Mallon free, Soper told her that she could not cook again, and she could not handle any food except her own. Mary Mallon promised.

In 1914, typhoid broke out again in a sanitarium where she worked, so she skipped out once more. In 1915, about forty-seven cases of typhoid were reported in Sloan Hospital (mostly among doctors and nurses), and they had just had a cook named Mary Brown, who fit Mallon's description.

Officials searched again in New Jersey, then Maine, Manhattan and Westchester County, New York. One night they caught her, although she was wearing a heavy veil, while carrying food to a sick friend. They placed her in isolation in North Brother Island.

Eight years later the city gave her a cottage, where she cooked her own food and was allowed guests. Although she an intelligent woman, she never quite understood what had happened to her.

She had a stroke, but lived six more years until November 11, 1938. Nine unidentified mourners came to her funeral.

As for the Islesboro, Maine connection, "The History of Islesboro, Maine 1893–1983" reports, "On the East Shore Frank Bond built Indian Head. Mr. Bond's house held too many sad memories. His little girl died there with typhoid fever. Their cook was a carrier, "Typhoid Mary," who came here with the J. Coleman Draytons, who lived in the Alpheus Pendleton house, and was eventually caught by the health officers."

A member of the Islesboro historical society told me what her mother had told her. In the attic of the Bond household was the helps' room and a big water tank. It was said that "Typhoid Mary" dipped her cup in the water tank whenever she was thirsty. The germ carried to the family that way, as well as through Mary's handling of their food.

'Tis a sad story of Mary Mallon.

"The Great One"

This article about World War I may be of interest, because it happened so long ago that few remember what we should know about it. Actually the military conflict began in Europe in 1914 and ended in 1918. It began between Austria-Hungry and Serbia, due to the assassination on June 28, 1914, of Archduke Francis Ferdinand, who was presumed to be heir to the throne, by Gavrilo Princip, a Serbian nationalist.

That incident led to a global war involving thirty-two nations. The Allies of twenty-eight countries, including Britain, France, Russia, Italy and the United States, opposed the Central Powers, which were Germany, Austria-Hungry, Turkey and Bulgaria.

The causes date back to the late nineteenth and into the twentieth centuries. As usual, the reasons were both political and economical. Germany, Italy and Belgium had all previously been divided in various parts in the 1800s, and it took a while for them to get their independence and unification. Germany became a great world power in 1871.

Even after that was resolved toward the end of the nineteenth century, there still seemed to be an economic conflict. Because of such tensions between 1871 and 1914, the nations in Europe kept large armies and also increased their navies. They armed themselves not only for self-defense, but also so that they would not be standing alone if war broke out. Between 1905 and 1914, there were many disturbances between various countries that threatened to bring about a European war.

United States President Woodrow Wilson gambled that he could maintain the right to trade with various powers without running the risk of war. However, Germany kept provoking the United States by sinking its ships, with lives and cargo lost. The episode most familiar seems to be the *Lusitania* in 1915. Wilson did not want war, but the Germans had resorted

CHRISTMAS JOYS

*When the Yuletide log is burning,
And the tree is gleaming bright,
Light a candle for the boy—
Who is fighting for the Right.*

Postcards were printed in World War I depicting a "dough boy." *Courtesy of the Camden History Center.*

to unrestricted submarine warfare, planning to defeat Britain. So on April 6, 1917, the United States declared war on Germany.

The Camden Surgical Dressings Committee worked throughout the summer of 1916 at the Camden Yacht Club, making seven thousand dressings. When it closed, the group moved to a vacant store in the Masonic block and continued. The members also made comfort bags for the soldiers, containing soap, socks, puzzles, pipes, etc., which were sent to the wounded French soldiers. Much of those, Camden shipped to two hospitals in France. Mrs. Mary Borden-Turner, daughter of William Borden of Camden, organized it.

The people in town felt the effect as food prices rose. Residents took part in a nationwide effort called Four Minute Men. People from Camden gave four-minute speeches to promote the sale of Liberty Bonds. For the second sale, Camden had a quota of $112,000.

A large "Welcome the Boys Home" parade took place in Camden on August 19, 1919.

Red Cross rooms became important as the war progressed. Surgical dressings and knitted goods constituted the bulk of the work here. Then a Junior Red Cross program started, and soon 150 people were involved.

The first draft of 178 men were called from Knox County, and the second in March of 1918 only required 11 men.

The flu epidemic, from which many young people died, tragically struck Camden. At the same time, we began hearing casualties of World War I: Russell Arey died of gunshot wounds on August 28, 1918, and Harold Heal on October 23, 1918. Camden's summer resident Henry Keep had been killed in action on October 5, as were Benjamin Lee II, Frank Jordan and Raymond Wellman.

The United States fought in the war only a short time, from April 6, 1917, to November 11, 1918, when the armistice was signed. People declared a holiday in Camden. Whistles blew from 8:45 a.m. to 10:00 p.m., and people held an impromptu parade. By noon a more formal celebration took place with the Camden Band, and there was a large bonfire with fireworks in the evening.

On August 19, 1919, after the boys had come home, a very large parade was held in town. The stores were all decorated with red, white and blue buntings, and it had to be one of the largest parades ever held in Camden. They called it the Welcome the Boys Home Parade.

The celebration started about 2:00 p.m. with the Camden and Vinalhaven Bands playing concerts in what is now the Village Green. All the church

Merchants decorated their stores for the welcoming parade.

bells rang at 3:30 p.m., and a half hour later the parade formed on Bay View Street. "Skip" Parsons led the parade on horseback. With all the floats prepared for the event, it was a mile long. After the parade, the former servicemen had dinner in the Opera House. In the evening, a large Carnival Dance was held in Post Office Square. Chestnut Street was roped off, and colored lights were strung over the dance area. One band played for the street dance, while another played for the dance in the Opera House. A great deal of community spirit went into the celebration.

After the war, fifty of the veterans formed the Arey-Heal Legion Post, which marched in every Memorial Day parade. The square where Mechanic, Elm, Main and Bay View come together was named the Arey-Heal Square. On May 31, 1920, the group dedicated the Memorial Oaks that had been planted on what is today the Camden Public Library grounds, in memory of Russell Arey, Harold Heal, Miles Dodge, Henry Keep and Benjamin Lee. The veterans raised a service flag at the Post Office containing 141 blue stars and 2 gold ones. In Rockport, they planted trees for those killed in action and placed flags from every country that had been fighting with us. Those flags are now at the Camden Area History Center.

We have been in several wars since, starting with World War II ("The Big One"), the one to end all wars, so they thought. Then came the Korean War, Vietnam, Desert Storm and now Iraqi Freedom.

Have you checked out Camden's new lovely granite Honor Roll in the Village Green that was dedicated on Memorial Day 2007? Have you thanked a veteran today?

Waterfront Fire

It happened on a Sunday afternoon about seventy-two years ago. To me it was not just any Sunday afternoon, because the date was May 19. I had nothing to do, so I walked downtown to buy an ice cream cone at Dougherty's Store (where Cappy's is now located). That would be my birthday celebration.

Smoke filled the air, and as I walked around the corner of Crockett's 5 & 10 Cent Store (where Camden National Bank is today), I found much more excitement than I had anticipated.

It seems that a blaze had been discovered in a frame storage building in the rear of the Bay View Street Garage (now Peter Ott's Restaurant). Leroy Alley had run to the alarm box on the corner near Brown's Market (now Camden Embroidery).

High winds had fanned the flames toward the large brick building once occupied by the Camden Anchor-Rockland Machine Company. Fire Chief Allen Payson knew by the looks of the flames and high winds from the north that Camden had troubles and needed help. He called the Rockland and Rockport Fire Departments, which rushed to aid our town.

I decided they didn't need me around, so I headed for home. Burned embers covered the waterfront and I could see them halfway home, as far as Limerock Street. The fire fed on the large frame building and contents from the Anchor Works building that was 175 feet by 60 feet. Next it went to the two-story office building, so all of these buildings were totally consumed.

Because the wind came from the north, many stores on Main and Bay View Streets were spared. But, of course, many small fires started on the roofs of the coal sheds belonging to P.G. Willey and George H. Thomas Fuel Company. Many of the wooden wharves, as far as the Camden Yacht Club, had fires starting.

A fire set the Anchor Works ablaze.

The Camden Public Landing was a gift to Camden.

Waterfront Fire

Thirteen lines of hose kept wetting down roofs of the Camden Herald Building, Bay View Street Garage, Ayer's Fish Market, Lamb's Machine Shop, J.H. Hobbs Lumber Company and the Marine Supply store. It began to rain, which helped the three fire departments prevent all the shingled roofs along the waterfront from burning.

By Wednesday, the fire department estimated the loss and damage to be about $50,000. The Camden Lumber Company's loss totaled $30,000, and the Anchor Works buildings owned by Isadore Gordon came to $10,000. None had been insured.

Several boats that had been moored along the waterfront were towed out of the danger zone. Included among them were *Alice May*, a schooner, and a powerboat of the Camden-Dark Harbor passenger line.

There had been a number of fires in that area during the previous year, and people felt the fires had been set intentionally. But this fact, to my knowledge, has never been proven.

It has been stated that some good comes out of all bad things that happen. In this case, the whole area was cleaned up, and thanks to Mary Louise Curtis Bok (Zimbalist), our Camden Public Landing came to be. That area is now beautiful and useful, and is enjoyed by many residents and tourists alike.

The Boston Boat

Until 1959, at the end of Sea Street, where condominiums are today, a business that fascinated all had that place in Camden history. Some Camden natives are still nostalgic when they speak of the "Boston Boat." A delightful way to travel between Boston and Bangor (or other coastal places) included a trip on the "Boston Boat." The travelers included salesmen, tourists, children going to summer camp, ordinary people or even the Gibson Girls, who summered on Seven Hundred Acre Island. Smaller boats met the steamboats and carried people to Maine islands in the bay.

The first steamboat ever to arrive in Penobscot Bay (and Camden) came in 1823, according to Robinson's *History of Camden and Rockport.* He writes,

> *Tradition says that it was with a good deal of trepidation that some people learned of her proposed trips into our harbor and some thought that she ought not be allowed to come here lest she frighten away all the fish, but as it has happened many times since, when objections have been made to some proposed innovation looking toward progress, the steamboats came just the same.*

Her name was the *Maine,* and she was commanded by Captain Daniel Lunt of Lincolnville. She connected at Bath with the steamer *Patent,* plying between that port and Boston. From Bath to Camden the fare was two dollars.

When the *Maine* first arrived in Camden, a salute from a cannon announced the fact, and a great multitude assembled at the shore to witness the approach of the new "Fultonian" craft. Many visited the vessel during its stay here.

The Sanford Steamship Co. (S.S. Co.) started in 1833 as the first line from Boston to Bangor. It ran for forty-nine years. The changes came as follows: in 1882 the Boston & Bangor S.S. Co. (B&B S.S. Co.); in 1902 the

Many people enjoyed going to the steamship wharf when the "Boston boats" arrived.

Eastern S.S. Co. (E.S.S. Co.); in 1912 Eastern S.S. Corp. (E.S.S. Corp.); and from 1917 until 1935, the Eastern S.S. Lines, Inc., (E.S.S.L. Inc.).

The sister ships *City of Rockland* and *City of Bangor*, both side-wheelers, were replaced by the *Camden* and the *Belfast*. They built *Camden*, a steel turbine steamer, at Bath Iron Works, and launched it on February 14, 1907. Her twin, *Belfast*, also was launched from Bath Iron Works in 1909. The length of both at the waterline was approximately 320 feet.

The steamers left Foster's Wharf in Boston promptly as the whistle blew at five o'clock in the afternoon, which gave three hours of daylight to enjoy sailing along the Massachusetts coast. Nahant, Salem, Marblehead and Gloucester successfully passed. Darkness set in just after the twin lights on Cape Ann. Early risers could see some beautiful views of the rockbound coast of Maine, between the Kennebec and Penobscot Rivers.

After that distance, the waters were smoother due to numerous islands that acted as breakwaters. About 3:00 a. m., the steamship passed Monhegan, Mosquito Island and Tenants Harbor before passing Whitehead Light.

Then it made its way through either of two channels to Owls Head and the Rockland Breakwater. It made a twenty-minute stop in Rockland in order to load either freight or people. The limekilns there lit up the coast.

As in most ports, folks from Camden gathered at the end of Sea Street, at the Steamship Wharf, around 7:30 a.m., when the "Boston Boat" arrived. As travelers collected their baggage, the porter would say, "All those passengers

The steamboat *Camden* was built in Bath, Maine.

what intended stopping at the beautiful village of the Penobscot [meaning Camden], please land on the upper deck stepping forward."

The most vivid memories I had as a small child seem to be the bright red carpet running down the twelve-foot gangway, lined on both sides with shiny brass spittoons. After unloading the passengers, baggage and freight reloaded, the boat left for Northport, Belfast, Bucksport and on to Bangor.

Although we are nostalgic about those steamers, some trips weren't all smooth sailing or without incident. At times the water could be very rough, making the steamer rock and roll. Numerous collisions occurred, due mostly to foggy conditions. On October 10, 1914, the *Belfast*, headed for Bangor, collided with the Camden-built *Alma A.E. Holmes* off Graves Light. Then on October 31, 1916, the steamer *Camden* ran into a fishing boat, *Arthur James*. The fishing boat sank and one life was lost, but the investigation did not find Captain Brown at fault.

We had extremely cold weather in the winter of 1917, and the Penobscot Bay froze over to Islesboro and beyond. Eight vessels from the Eastern Steamship Co. could not get out of Camden Harbor. What an unusual sight that must have been!

The following year, *Camden* and *Belfast* changed from the Boston to Bangor run to serve the Boston to New York trip. During that time, the *City of Rockland* and the *City of Bangor* replaced them temporarily.

Fire totally destroyed the Camden Steamship Wharf on August 1, 1924. It was rebuilt the following fall and winter, and it was completed in 1925.

In 1927, the *Camden* ran on a rock at the entrance to Camden Harbor. They had to quarantine the *Belfast* in Boston the next year, due to an outbreak of smallpox among the crew. All crew members and one hundred passengers had to be vaccinated and the vessel fumigated before it could resume service.

In August of 1928, the steamer *Camden* rescued a Camden man who had jumped overboard just outside Camden Harbor. Also the *Camden*, on September 2, saved two men who clung to a capsized boat near Salem, Massachusetts.

Eventually, in 1933, the steamer *Camden* had installed a sonar-type device to notify the captain and crew of objects not visible in the fog. They located the siren on the roof of the pilothouse, with two electronic ears detecting echoes from anything in its path.

All good things must come to an end, and so the services of the Boston Boats became no longer useful. Trucks and automobiles had gained popularity, and the Great Depression had an impact on business.

Captain Alfred E. Rawley, master of the *Belfast* for twenty-two years, left Camden for the final trip on December 27, 1935.

The Colonial Lines purchased the *Camden* and renamed it *Comet*. Also they purchased the *Belfast*, giving it the new name *Arrow*. The ships became sound steamers until World War II, when they were called into the service of their country as troop transports, operating out of Honolulu.

When the war ended, they were laid up for a while until the Asia Development Corporation bought *Comet* (*Camden*) for Chinese service. Renamed *Ya Sung*, it is reported that the Chinese Communists captured it for scrap.

The *Arrow* (*Belfast*) wrecked while being towed in 1945, and was grounded off Oak Park, Washington. Buried deep in the mud, the masts were salvaged, and her whistle came back to Belfast to a sardine cannery. It still sounded off in 1968.

Local businessmen purchased the Eastern Steamship Wharf in Camden. They sold it in 1941 to Camden Shipbuilding & Marine Railways Co., which used it as a mold loft during World War II. After the war, the Camden Cabin Company owned it.

In 1951, the Helioffs purchased the wharf for a lobster holding and packing plant. Three years later, due to stress and strain, the center section collapsed, and eighteen thousand pounds of lobsters went back to their natural habitat.

Eventually the piling began to give way. Due to the "flotsam and jetsam," the wharf was declared a menace to navigation. At a special town meeting on May 11, 1959, the townspeople voted to burn it. During the next three days, much of the salvageable lumber was removed. On May 15, Mr. Andrew Sides, a former vice-president of the Eastern Steamship Lines, had the honor of lighting the oil-soaked ropes.

It burned for three days, hating to "give up the ghost." Pilings still standing were removed, along with so many fond memories.

The pilings had to be removed after the steamship wharf was burned.

Oakland Park

Today it is nearly impossible to think of any place where families could spend all day Sunday at no charge. But beginning in 1902, Oakland Park began, free of charge, with just a ride on the electric trolley car.

It all began when the trolley cars became the principal mode of transportation so vital to Camden, Rockport, Rockland and Thomaston. The service started in 1892 and ran for thirty-nine years. The line left Camden from Main Street in front of today's House of Logan, and continued up Union Street, the main highway. The company had both open and closed cars to accommodate the weather. The car barns and power station had buildings on what old-timers refer to as Power House Hill in Glen Cove.

The trolley service also placed waiting shelters conveniently along its route in several places for the travelers. The one in Camden could hold about thirty people. There were two smaller ones in Rockport; one held twenty and the other only ten. At Ballard Park and Oakland Park there were open shelters. Rockland needed more, so they located one with a capacity for ten at the junction of Waldo Avenue and Camden Street. Another in the Rankin Block, but the one in the company office building, held one hundred trolley travelers. One in Rockland was at the junction of Park and Union Streets for twelve people, plus there were several others. The one in Thomaston Village held twenty people, and another was at the upper corner of the junction to South Warren. The Warren Village waiting room had a capacity for twenty.

The fare between each zone began at five cents. In 1918 it increased to six cents, and went up again to seven cents in 1919. Seven zones came between Camden and Warren. In 1924, the fare increased to ten cents and remained at that price until the end, around 1931.

This shows the lovely entrance to Oakland Park.

At Oakland Park there was a pond that at one time had an alligator in it.

This was the attractive bandstand where band concerts were held.

Unbelievable as it may seem, the trolley company made enough money to create and maintain Oakland Park in 1902. The park encompassed seventy-two acres that included a casino, a pond, dance hall, restaurants, bandstand and a baseball diamond. The Rockland, Thomaston and Camden Street Railway purchased an alligator in 1916 for an added attraction. The suffragette movement held a rally at Oakland Park. It must have helped, as women were allowed to vote not long afterward. Can you imagine all the families that spent their free time in such a wonderful place as this, free of charge?

That is correct. Rockland, Thomaston and Camden Street Railway charged nothing to enjoy Oakland Park. They had schedules of distances and running times, which listed Camden to Oakland Park as 4.5 miles, taking twenty-three minutes to get there. Park Street in Rockland to Oakland Park was 3.5 miles and took fifteen minutes for the ride.

Only two accidents occurred in the thirty-nine years of the trolley cars' existence. One happened on August 12, 1911, when car #22—which was carrying schoolchildren to Warren after a day at Oakland Park—met car #17 head on near O'Brien's siding in Warren. The accident killed one person and injured six more. The explanation claimed that there was a misunderstanding of orders given by the railway superintendent.

Although the trolleys no longer existed, nor did Oakland Park per se, dances were still running in 1939, until World War II came along. After the war ended, three young men purchased the place and continued the dances. What a romantic place, near the water's edge, and with a large ball of mirrors constantly revolving and sending spots of color all around the dance floor. One might relate it to strobe lights of today, but a little more subtle. Later, the dance hall turned into a roller-skating rink, as that sport had become popular.

Then a young Camden man, Howard Dearborn, became the sole owner for the rest of his life. The dance hall is now a motel and there are lovely cabins by the water. The two entrances remain off Route 1, near the Off Shore Restaurant.

Oakland Park is a busy place today in the tourist season, but it still holds fond memories of happy days gone by.

Camden Harbor

By the time you read this article, beautiful Camden Harbor will have been dredged again of the sand, etc., that filters in. The moorings will all have been removed, and the chains inspected and replaced. The Camden Harbor Committee watches over all activities of the harbor and has many ordinances by which to abide.

From the Gulf of Mexico to the Bay of Fundy, only two places exist where the mountains meet the sea: Mount Desert Island and Camden, Maine. That probably is the reason why Camden Harbor has been talked and written about for three hundred years. It snuggles at the foot of Mount Megunticook and Mount Battie. Nearly all refer to the harbor as a haven, perhaps even a heaven, for the tourists and yachtsmen who frequent it each summer.

Many of us "natives" can tell you of the many changes, and most of them are for the better. Explorers such as Martin Pring in 1603, Captains George Weymouth and John Smith sailed by. Most historians do not believe they entered the harbor, except Captain Weymouth, but all did use it for a landmark.

Camden's first settler, James Richards, his wife Betty and their African cook sailed into the harbor in May of 1769 to live here. When there were 331 inhabitants, they decided they needed a town government, so Camden became incorporated in 1791 as the seventy-second town in Maine.

As the town grew, steamships ran between Boston and Bangor, with the wharf on the east side of the harbor, where the condominiums are in the middle of Wayfarer.

A little to the east of that point is land called "the Bean Yard." Beginning in 1855, Hodgman and Glover had a shipyard for a few years, and in 1875 Holly Bean had his famous yard in the same location. He built about seventy-one vessels in all, including the second five-master and first six-

Camden Harbor snuggles beneath its two mountains.

This is a bird's-eye view of the Harbor.

master ever built. Later his son, Robert Bean, had a yard there until about 1920. Now the land belongs to Wayfarer Marine Corporation.

During World War II, the current Wayfarer property on the whole east side of the harbor became a shipyard for the war effort, constructing about thirty vessels over a three-year span for the United States Navy, the Maritime Commission and for Great Britain, under the lend-lease program.

At its peak during the war, Camden Shipbuilding & Marine Railways Company, Inc., employed fifteen hundred men and women in two shifts. They constructed minesweepers (AMc), troop transports (APc), coal barges (MCc) and rescue salvage tugs (ATR). After the war, Camden Shipbuilding built pleasure yachts until 1963.

Since then, many buildings have burned, the coal shed has been torn down, the old dock and loose pilings have been removed and a new dock has been built. The red sheds at the head of the harbor have all been removed, except for one that was repaired/rebuilt. Many improvements have taken place since 1980. It is an up-to-date shipyard designed to service, repair and store yachts of all sizes. The outdated railways no longer need to be in service, because in 1999 Wayfarer Marine Corporation purchased a 110-ton mobile boat hoist from Italy, known as an ASCOM.

The "head of the harbor" once had small boatyards, when High Street went to the water's edge. The town built Atlantic Avenue in 1880.

A first-class hotel, Ocean House, sat where the Camden Public Library is today. After its construction in 1928, Mrs. Edward Bok purchased the adjoining land and hired the well-known landscape architect Fletcher Steele to design the amphitheater. She purchased the property across the road and hired the Olmsted firm to design Harbor Park.

As we continue to circle the harbor, there is the Camden Public Landing, with the cascading falls at the foot of Megunticook River. That area formerly had more industry than beauty. The Aldens established the Camden Anchor Works, where black smoke poured from the place both night and day, as they forged anchors that traveled on vessels around the world. The triphammers rang out, echoing over the water.

In the very early days, Chestnut Street extended to the water's edge, so there were shipyards all along the water. Bay View Street was built in 1866. At one time, there were about ten limekilns along the area, as far as the present Camden Yacht Club property of today. Cyrus H.K. Curtis chose that prime spot on the harbor and built the yacht club in the early 1900s. He presented it to the inhabitants of the town of Camden in 1926.

The businesses that dominated Bay View Street about 1935 were A.H. Parson's Plumbing, the Bay View Garage, lumberyards, fuel companies, a fish market, a grocery store, a restaurant and I. Nee Lee's laundry.

If you remember (or can imagine) what lumber- and coal yards looked like, then you know that Bay View Street today is much more attractive with its nice shops.

The whole perimeter of Camden Harbor has been greatly improved over the years. It is considered "a thing of beauty and a sight to behold."

People call this the prettiest spot in Maine.

The Great Imposter

On February 14, 1957, the residents of North Haven got the surprise they didn't expect. Two state police detectives, James Milligan and Millard Nickerson, arrived courtesy of the U.S. Coast Guard. Without an automobile, they found that the island had one taxi service, which they took and headed for the school. Their mission was to arrest Ferdinand Waldo Demara, an exceptionally brilliant man, but later known for all his escapades in the movie *The Great Imposter*, starring Tony Curtis.

We had heard on the mainland about the wonderful teacher on North Haven, who did everything with the students; reportedly he appeared odd at times, but he wanted to help the poor. He led a Boy Scout troop. Among other things, he also played jolly Santa Claus, being large and plump. The alias that he went by on the island was Martin Godgart.

Many wondered why he picked the island of North Haven, when with his abilities and credentials he could have taught in cities with a much larger salary. Later the people learned that he was an impeccable imposter.

If you read his biography by Robert Crichton, *The Great Imposter*, published about 1959, Demara is described as a self-destructive genius with a remarkable ability to assume the identities of others in order to kill off parts of himself. He called himself "a rotten man." His got his thrills by stealing a man's credentials to "become" him, and then being able to impress anyone to get any job he wanted, until he tired of one episode and began another.

He began as a teenager who left home and joined a monastery. That was not his style, as he loved to talk. His next try was in the army. He stole the records of his army buddy; later, he again entered another monastery.

After December 7, 1941, when Japan bombed Pearl Harbor, he joined the navy and planned to climb the ranks quickly. In order to do this, he set fire to a wastebasket in the commander's office. During the commotion he stole stationery. He then faked a suicide by drowning. The navy did catch up with him while he was acting as a dean in a college. He served time in a military prison.

After his jail time, he came up with papers to show he was a cancer researcher. He was hired at Notre Dame Normal School, as Dr. Cecil Hamann. He met up with a Canadian doctor who wished to practice in the United States. So Demara said that he would take the doctor's credentials and of course get them in the right hands...his hands. They got him a commission as a surgeon who had graduated from Harvard.

He became the doctor of a ship headed for Korea. On the ship, the captain had three impacted teeth, so Demara looked up the procedure in a book before pulling them. He later patched up a group of South Korean soldiers, removing shrapnel, etc. He also removed a bullet that was located near a soldier's heart. Just think: he had no medical training.

He stayed in Korea as a well-liked doctor. Demara ran into trouble when the real Canadian doctor began reading about what he (himself) was supposed to be doing in Korea. He requested that the navy investigate the man, which they did.

Demara tried very hard to convince the officers that they had made a mistake, and he really was a doctor. He would get very upset and drunk, especially when he received letters and packages from "Catherine," who said she loved him no matter who he was. Finally he demanded to be released at once under threat of embarrassing the Canadian navy.

The Royal Canadian Naval Headquarters released the shortest statement ever, stating, "Ferdinand Waldo Demara, alias Dr. Cyr will be discharged at Esquimalt late today, November 21, 1951."

He was at rock bottom again in money and ego. So he sold his story to *Life* magazine for $2,500. After beginning treatment through Alcoholics Anonymous, he met the right people, obtained more credentials and landed a job in the Huntsville prison as warden, where an inmate recognized him from the magazine articles. Once again, officials knew he was guilty, but he was able to convince them they were wrong, at least long enough for him to get away. So Texas dropped their charges, just as the military had. They didn't want him in Texas either. He was excellent at planning plots to land big jobs, and by many complicated ways he succeeded.

Mr. Demara was working in New York when he heard about the town of North Haven, Maine, needing a teacher very badly. Well, he had credentials for that tucked away, and he got the job.

He became friendly with a family who had two boys in school. One day he pulled a loaded gun from his pocket to show the boys, just as their mother came into the room. She had wondered for quite some time about him. He showed the pictures of himself in *Life* magazine, so the mother sent for that issue of *Life* and realized he really was an imposter. After obtaining his fingerprints from a glass, they were sent to Augusta for testing.

When the detectives arrived, he asked, "What took you so long?" Again he was put on two years' probation and asked to go far, far away.

The people in North Haven, Maine, learned that Demara became a teacher twice more, joined another monastery and even became a minister. It took an exceptional mind to plan all the schemes he had thought up in a lifetime, but he was a troubled soul.

It was difficult to believe that a man who was so brilliant wanted to use his strange ability simply to fool people. It was only by reading Crichton's book and seeing the movie that we learned more than just the rumors that had circulated here. Recently, after many years, I reread *The Great Imposter*, and still found myself fascinated by the man with a mind that even psychologists and psychiatrists couldn't figure out.

George W. Wells

The first six-masted schooner ever built came out of the Holly M. Bean Yard in Camden, Maine. They constructed it where Wayfarer Marine Corporation now stores boats, in the so-called "Bean Yard." Mr. George W. Wells happened to be the largest financial backer of the vessel, which was said to cost $120,000.

John Wardwell, known as a successful designer and master builder, designed it in 1899. Mr. Wardwell had been born in Penobscot, Maine, and moved to Stockton in 1864, becoming foreman later in the N.G. Hitchborn yard. Twenty-one years later, he moved to Camden, before moving on to Rockland to be the master builder in the Cobb-Butler yard.

From the *Camden Herald* on August 14, 1900:

> *Ten thousand persons saw the launching this afternoon of the mammoth six-master,* George W. Wells, *the largest schooner in the world.*
>
> *The launching was witnessed by one of the largest crowds which ever gathered for such an event. Among the unique features of the occasion was the christening ceremony, which was performed by Miss May Wells, who scattered white roses upon the bow of the vessel as she started down the ways, and at the same time let loose a flock of white pigeons. Miss Wells is the daughter of the man for whom the vessel was named.*
>
> *The ceremonies were concluded with a dance in the Opera House this evening given by the young society women of Camden. The officers of the battleships,* Kearsarge *and* Indiana, *which were in the harbor, were among the guests.*
>
> *A year or more ago, when it was announced that Capt. John G. Crowley of Taunton, Mass., was to build a six-masted vessel people laughed at him. It was his idea to give the shipping world the largest vessel ever built.*

This shows only the stern of the vessel *George W. Wells*.

A shot of the six-master *George W. Wells* under construction.

The keel for this great craft was laid April 1 last year and so rapidly has the work progressed that she is practically finished as to hull. The launching made the occasion of a great demonstration in Camden because it is not every little seaport town that leads the world in her class, and not often that any shipyard sends overboard $120,000 worth of material in one lump.

Nowadays a big schooner is no novelty for there are plenty of colossal four-masters and five-masters have long ceased to attract attention, but a six-master of 2750 tons register and having a carrying capacity of rising 5000 tons is something that people wonder at.

The George W. Wells *is of magnificent dimensions. On the keel she is 303 feet, 11 inches long; 325 feet length on top; 48 feet 6 inches beam and 23 feet depth. She has two full decks, with a poop four feet deep extending from the taffrail to the forward hatch, and a set of beams in the lower hold forward braced with hanging fore and aft knees.*

The topmast is 58 feet in length, jibboom 75 feet, driver boom 72 feet. She is fitted out with all modern appliances. Her ground tackle is of the heaviest description, one anchor weighing 8280 lbs., and the other 7500 lbs., and attached to each is 800 fathoms of 2½ inch chain. All her fastenings are 1³⁄₈ and 1¼ inch iron.

Her frame is white oak throughout and all her ceiling and planking is hard pine. The garboards are 8 inches thick. Her ceiling to the lower deck beam is 12 and 14 inches thick and between decks, 10x14 and 12x14.

The six lower masts are splendid sticks of Oregon pine each 119 feet long. The masts are named as follows: foremast, mainmast, mizzenmast, spankermast, jiggermast and drivermast.

The vessel will carry 12,000 square yards of the heaviest duck in the following pieces: driver, jigger, spanker, mizzen, main and fore sails; six gaff topsails of the same descriptive designation, driver, jigger, spanker, mizzen and main topmast, staysails and five jibs.

The cabins and staterooms are finished in ash, sycamore and cherry and supplied with steam heat, baths, hot and cold water, electric bells and a telephone to the galley and engine house.

While she is a large vessel, she is also a handsome craft being much the best looking of all the schooners afloat. Her great length takes away every appearance of bulkiness as she lies on the ways in the yard. She looks like an immense yacht with her sharp bow, clean run aft and graceful lines all over.

Twelve vessels like her ranged in line would occupy a mile of pier frontage, from the tip of her driver boom to the tip of her jibboom is about 425 feet. She can carry as much coal in one load as can three of the big steam colliers of the Philadelphia and Reading Railroad, and about twice as much as is carried by the first five-masted vessel ever built, the Gov. Ames. *A schooner that would have been called large twenty years ago would not load enough coal to ballast this giant of the Camden yard.*

The Wells *will be commanded by Capt. Arthur Crowley of Taunton, Mass., who is at present commander of the five-master,* John B. Prescott, *owned by the Crowleys. Capt. Crowley is only 30 years old, but has been to sea since his boyhood. Another six-masted schooner of about the same size as* Wells *is now being built in Bath and will be launched within a few weeks.*

The *Wells* was a beautiful vessel under full sail.

The Hole in the Donut

Camden, Maine, has been known for many things, but one is very unique. When Elizabeth Foxwell became Camden's first secretary of the chamber of commerce, she felt that Camden's Captain Hanson Crockett Gregory deserved permanent recognition for inventing the hole in the donut, and she began fundraising for a statue of the captain.

It seemed that when the captain was but fifteen years of age, in 1847, he asked his mother while she was making fried cakes why the centers were so soggy. She said for some reason they just never cooked. So young Gregory knocked out the soggy center of a fried cake before his mother cooked it, and that became the world's first "ring" donut. That is the true story according to Fred Crockett, whose parents were both related to Captain Gregory.

There were other stories floating around about how he made his discovery. One told that when he was a captain, he lost six of his crew overboard after they had eaten the soggy fried cakes. The weight made the men sink to the bottom before they could be rescued. (Perhaps that is why donuts are sometimes called "sinkers.") So he began to think about it and punched a hole in a fried cake with a belaying pin.

Another version stated that the captain tried to eat fried cakes while at the wheel of his ship. A storm came up and he had to put the fried cake on the wheel's spokes in order to use both hands at the wheel.

More stories picked up from there. Someone from New Hampshire said a lumberman invented the hole in the donut.

Alton Blackington loved lore and legends. While visiting his grandfather, Henry A. Ellis, in Cape Cod, "Blackie" told him the story and said, "We can do better than that." So they came up with this: Henry's grandmother Sally was a Wampanoag. When Henry was a young man, Grandma told him the story of how the hole in the donut had been invented. She said that a Pilgrim woman fried cakes in a large kettle over an outdoor fire. Two of her Indian ancestors wanted a couple of those cakes, so one aimed an arrow at the kettle, but it missed and drove a hole through the cake. It fried without a soggy center.

These stories began appearing in many newspapers like the *Christian Science Monitor, Portland Telegram, Deer Isle Messenger, Bedford Standard Times*, the *Camden Herald* and magazines like *Down East, Smithsonian, Cape Cod Magazine* and *Yankee*. Others got into the act. The Pillsbury Cooking School created a donut that was one foot in diameter.

A lively correspondence flowed constantly between Betty Foxwell from Camden's Chamber and Henry Ellis, a lawyer from Cape Cod. About three thick folders of letters were exchanged with great humor, and are now on file in the Camden Public Library archives. Imagine all of this caused by a hole in the donut! But it was excellent publicity for both Camden, Maine, and Cape Cod, Massachusetts.

In October of 1941, the Dunking Association asked Camden and Cape Cod to debate the issue in New York's Hotel Astor. Fred Crockett, related to Captain Hanson Crockett Gregory, debated for Camden, with the lawyer Ellis arguing for the Cape. A high medicine man from the Wampanoag tribe showed up to swear by the Great Spirit that the Cape Cod story was the truth. He took front and center stage, in his Indian headpiece and all. It certainly got the judges' attention, but it did not convince them.

The judges chosen were Elsa Maxwell (noted columnist), Franklin Adams (journalist) and Clifton Fadiman (writer); all were well known at that time. After the "great debate," they declared Fred Crockett (and Camden) the winner.

Captain Gregory's home on the Old County Road in Glen Cove (once part of Camden) is now the Nativity Lutheran Church. Facing the parking lot is a plaque placed in November 2, 1947, commemorating the captain.

There have been two donut festivals. The first one was sponsored by the Camden-Rockport Chamber of Commerce on August 17, 1957. The second one was held on June 11, 1994, organized by Mary Jane Schepers and Karen Weed. Proceeds went toward the new restrooms on the Public Landing.

The Camden Public Library had a program last year for the young children to write an essay on who invented the hole in the donut. Fred Crockett was one of several judges. After the essays were judged, Amy Hand, one of the children's librarians, had the kids make donuts right there and treated them to their cooking.

Really this story is not complete without new dunking rules 1942–43, adopted by the National Dunking Association, which read as follows:

Fred Crockett was the winner of the "hole in the donut" debate. *Courtesy of Camden Area History Center, from Fred Crockett Collection.*

There are two important changes in the new rules. As you all know, the present rules advocate the donut being held between the thumb and forefinger, with the other three fingers pointing daintily upward. Well, this position, graceful as it is, has been open to some criticism. Critics claim that the three upward-pointing fingers add a touch of studied elegance not keeping with the democratic nature of dunking. Your executive committee has considered the question fully and carefully, and find some foundation for the complaints. The Upward-pointing fingers can look rather highbrow.

Therefore, to avoid any possible stigma of appearing high-hat, while still maintaining the dignity of dunking, we proclaim that the correct position for the fingers hereafter will be as follows: the thumb forefinger holding the donut as usual—but the tree other fingers held together and parallel with the forefinger! This pose, you will find, is natural, easy and attractive. Do not forget it. And tell other dunkers about it!

The second important change is in the immersion of the donut in the beverage used for dunking. Our present rule provides for the dipping of the donut into the beverage, then the rhythmic swishing of the donut therein in a circular motion. Unfortunately the circular motion sometimes—very rarely, but sometimes—causes a cup too full of liquid to overflow slightly. This is hardly noticeable, but to insure a maximum of fastidiousness and absolutely no spilling, it is recommended that hereafter the donut be swished in the cup in a square motion, slowly and gently. This technique has been tested with innumerable donuts by research experts within our organization, and has been found to be utterly satisfactory.

The next time you are eating or dunking a donut, you will have something about which to think.

Hello, Rockport, Maine

Isn't it about time to write something about beautiful Rockport, Maine? Before this article begins, I have to say one *little* thing that bothers me *BIG*. Every time I go by the sign "Leaving Rockport, settled in 1768" and then come to the sign that reads "Entering Camden, settled in 1769," I have to wonder how these two facts can both be true: Rockport was originally part of Camden, and the first settler came to Camden in May of 1769; just a few months after that, the first settler arrived in Rockport.

Back in the beginning, or once upon a time, Camden included many places. But the two larger sections were known as "the Harbor" (Camden) and "Goose River" (Rockport). The latter derived its name because one of the early settlers found the nest of a wild goose on a rock at Hosmer's Pond, so he named it Goose Pond. Since the pond's source is the river, they called that "Goose River."

Other sections received their own post offices: West Camden (now West Rockport) in 1834, Rockville in 1853, Clam Cove (now Glen Cove) in 1892 and Simonton's Corner had a post office from 1894 to 1901. As it lasted only seven years, there couldn't have been much mail passing through.

At the very first town meeting, residents voted to pay a Goose River man, Robert Thorndike, three pounds to build a pound on Peter Ott's property, with Ott as keeper. This would let the hogs run at large with rings, and sheep without a shepherd. The pen had to be tight enough to stop pigs as small as one month old.

At the next meeting, Captain William McGlathery of the Harbor organized his own group to put through an appropriation of £159 to build a new bridge over Camden's Megunticook River; of course, Captain McGlathery was to be the builder. This proposal took the Goose River group by surprise, so they called a special meeting reducing the amount

Goose River runs into Rockport Harbor.

to £12, 123 shillings, and changed the specifications so exact that poor McGlathery lost his shirt on the contract. Another story had it that he built the bridge too high and frail, so they would not pay him. Later they voted to pay him £20, and said that was the amount due from him for highway tax, wiping the slate clean.

Goose River seemed rural in character, and farming was the common trade. The Harbor kept advancing socially and economically. (Oh, if they could only see it today, advancing to the point where "natives" worry about paying taxes on their property.)

In 1812, the two sections did join forces against the British. Paul Thorndike sailed a privateer, a vessel owned privately but manned by the government in time of war. The British captured him and insisted on knowing of American defenses. He quite honestly replied, "Every stump is a place of defense, and every rock pile a fortification." Therefore, the British became nervous every time they saw a stump or rock pile, and soon went back to their vessels.

In later years, Camden had vessel buildings, grogshops and mills. Goose River village had but eighteen dwellings, and the only industry was a saltworks on Beauchamp Point. The major building consisted of the Granite Block, which housed a general store and post office. Because of the darkness inside, it was supposedly called a "hole in the wall."

The Granite Block looks today as it did when it was built many years ago.

Things began to change in 1838, when William Carleton moved his businesses from the Harbor to Goose River. Those businesses included a store, vessel building and lime industry. Then Hobbs and Pitts had a business cutting ice in the Lily Pond. Gilbert Eells began building vessels, such as the 140-ton *Lucy Blake*.

William Carleton died in 1840 and his son, Samuel Dexter Carleton, went into business with Joshiah Norwood building many vessels. They had a fine master builder, John Pascal, and between 1844 and 1892 they built sixty-two vessels, including the great *Frederick Billings*. At that time, it was the largest vessel built anywhere, but unfortunately it blew up with a load of nitrate.

About 1852, the name Goose River changed to Rockport. Rockland wasn't happy about it because it sounded too much like their name, which they hadn't had for very long.

I don't want to stir up trouble between Camden and Rockport, because I think after many years it has been forgotten. The Harbor, at town meeting, wanted to put in streets because of the tourists. Goose River wanted an iron bridge over the river instead. You can imagine the arguments at town meetings then. Not much went on for excitement or entertainment, so town meetings spiced it up a bit.

It seemed that the Harbor wanted to split the towns, whereas Rockport did not want to divide. The fight went to the House of Representatives in Augusta and was passed by the Senate. So in February of 1891, they became two towns. One legislator said, "You should be celebrating a centennial, instead of suing for a divorce." If you care to read the act that describes the boundaries of the separation, look in Robinson's *History of Camden and Rockport*.

When I was a child (several years ago) they were still saying, "Rockport paddywhackers live on soda crackers." The reply heard was, "Camden bum lives on rum." I haven't heard that for a while, and the two towns love each other now. They say, however, to step aside if someone says to a Rockporter, "Oh yes, I know where Rockport is. It is quite near Camden, isn't it?"

The boundary markers between Camden and Rockport are strange on Union Street. Rockport begins by the arch on the left-hand side leaving Camden. But on the right-hand side of the road, the marker is just beyond the Megunticook House by the entrance to the Carleton Cemetery. I understand that is because a Rockport man owned the lime business where the Transfer Station is today, so Camden either gave or sold that property to Rockport.

Joe Seagull

About one or two generations back, a popular businessman, George H. Thomas, used "Joe Seagull" in his advertisements. Surely Joe has gone to "gull heaven," but he left behind many relatives. They continue to watch over Camden, its village and harbor, but the job is more demanding, as the population back then totaled 3,554, but today it is 5,254. Not only are there 1,700 more residents, but there are many more tourists as well.

The young Joe Seagull perches on the Elm Street School. He doesn't fear the lead paint, and perhaps even doubts it, as so many youngsters have gone through that school since it was built in 1869. Joe never heard of any child getting lead poisoning.

While he is there, he cannot help but be fascinated by all the automobiles going through the stop sign. Oh, here is one that stops. But even though cars are coming over School Street it continues on through. Even Joe knows that STOP means STOP and not to GO until no one is coming. He notices that these offenders do not all bear out-of-state plates either. Who would ever expect a sign there anyway? Well, it must be the Maine Department of Transportation's fault. With good intentions, they probably wanted to slow down the traffic coming into Camden.

Joe Seagull gets bored with it all and flies down to sit on Rite-Aid's store. He notices that a story has been built above the store, but looking in the windows he sees nothing. Apartments are so scarce in Camden that this unused space would be a great find. Too bad to waste it, but maybe it is a Rite-Aid policy.

A tour bus has stopped at the Village Green, and another and here comes one more, but there is no room at the Green right now. A parade of seniors departs for the stores. He knows they will go to the Village Shop to buy some candy and maybe ice cream from Boynton's before it is time to leave again.

Joe Seagull himself keeps an eye on Camden.

The Garden Club spends hours fixing and watering the plants there, so Joe hopes they will be careful of them.

Well, just look at the congestion at the post office. Automobiles have their back-up lights on, but other drivers only have time to stop if they want that parking spot. What happened to the manners and politeness that old Joe Seagull used to watch? Maybe parents just don't have time to teach them, as they are so busy earning money to spend on their children, who must have what their schoolmates have. Joe doesn't quite understand why name-brand logos make the apparel any better (just more expensive). They get just as dirty dragging on the ground.

As the gull moves on, he chooses the Travelers' Building because it is the tallest one on the east side of Main Street. Well, someone is invading his fly zone space with bubbles, where Mechanic, Elm, Bay View and Main Streets meet. That adds a little excitement to the area, and he hears a gentleman singing as he walks along, "I'm forever blowing bubbles."

A shot of the Elm Street School when it was first built; it is still used as a school today.

The Veteran's Honor Roll has been added to the lovely Village Green.

One gets this view toward the harbor from the amphitheater.

Will ya look at that? A pretty young thing in her convertible does a U-turn right in the middle on Main Street, with all that traffic. She made it, but if she keeps that up, she may never know the pleasures of growing old or ever receiving her Social Security check. She won't have to worry about choosing between food or medicine.

Joe Seagull doesn't bother to turn around and look toward the Public Landing. He certainly has heard a lot about it lately, but the excitement probably won't begin until 9:00 p.m., so maybe he will return then.

He also has heard much in the summer about the Camden Public Library grounds, so he goes to overlook that. What a mess of cigarette butts by the wall near the beautiful Children's Garden. The ones who "hang out" are not old enough to smoke, so it must be the people who love that library. But if they love it, why would they use it and abuse it with trash, cigarette butts and trampled ground, wearing out the grass? Some say the young ones caused it, but he has heard many parents say, "Not MY child."

Joe Seagull overhears much that goes on in town. He heard one parent say to another, "Do you think $300 per week is enough allowance for a child?" Joe thinks, "Sure it is. All he has to do is have the $20 bills broken up into $5 and he can acquire a habit that will ruin him for life. Tell him or her to get a job, so they will have something important to do and learn the value of money."

When you see Joe Seagull fly over, just remember he is very observant and hears it all. He realizes that times have changed since old Joe was around, but he still loves Camden, no matter what.

Lazy, Hazy Days of Summer

Before school closed for the summer, I had the interesting experience of speaking to a seventh-grade class about "the good old days." They really listened very closely as I told them about the days when Mary E. Taylor was a strict but wonderful teacher and the grade school principal, not just the name of a building on Knowlton Street. They had sincere compassion for me because I grew up in the Great Depression, when no one had much money or toys. They couldn't imagine what we children could do for fun.

It was great to grow up in those times, when you had to use your imagination. We did not have anyone kind enough to build us a skateboard park, but we did not miss it because skateboards hadn't been invented.

No parents allowed their children to "hang out" in the beautiful parks in Camden. Our fun was playing in our neighborhood with friends who lived nearby. I suppose going out with a jar to catch lightning bugs, thinking if we caught enough of them we would have a flashlight, was rather dumb, but it was fun.

We played kick-the-can and allee, allee-in free. We all walked down Bay View Street to the Camden Yacht Club every evening, just to hear them fire the cannon as they lowered the flag. The members did not mind us there, as we had been brought up to respect everyone's property.

We enjoyed the hike to Maiden's Cliff to see the cross placed there in memory of little Eleanora French, who had fallen from the spot many years before. We also loved to climb Mount Battie, either up over the face of it or the "back way." No, the road was not there. It seemed steep in places, but when we reached the top, we sat around and ate our picnic lunch. There were usually some grownups who joined us. From Mount Megunticook and Mount Battie, the view was, and still is, spectacular.

From Maiden's Cliff, one has a view of Megunticook Lake.

Sherman's Point used to be a favorite picnic area for families.

Sherman's Point belonged to the town of Camden. No houses had been built there. Local families looked forward to picnicking on the Point. We were fortunate. We had friends in the neighborhood who came every summer to visit their grandmother. Their grandfather had a dinghy that he sometimes let us use. He kept it tied at the Public Landing. We would gather our supplies to take with us for the day's outing. We took a black iron frying pan, a few raw potatoes, Moxie and candy bars and the boys always carried a jackknife. We all had a line with a hook on it and some angleworms. I insisted on carrying a compass, because every sailor carried a compass, and it might become foggy between the Public Landing and Sherman's Point. Yes, we could read a compass.

Boarding the twelve-foot skiff, we had to be careful not to "rock the boat." We had been reminded of this over and over and over again. However, one of us would always lose our balance on purpose, for the excitement of rocking the others a little.

After agreeing upon who would sit where, our hooked and baited lines went overboard. Full of excitement and anticipation, we waited to see who would get the first tug on his line. Anyone caught flounders easily in those days. But we two girls would scream and giggle, as our brothers had to remove the floppy fish from the hooks. They would flip and flop, splashing us all.

We took turns rowing, and that meant changing places in the boat and rocking it some more. Sometimes it seemed that we pulled too hard on one oar and would be going in circles. Finally we would reach Sherman's Point. The next step was to beach the boat, tie it to a tree and unload our supplies.

If the tide happened to be low, we could jump rocks to Mouse Island and picnic there. The boys would build the fire, behead the flounders and remove their fins and tails. We girls had the job of peeling the raw potatoes. The aroma of frying flounders and cooking the slices of raw potatoes was something no gourmet cook today could imagine.

As we enjoyed our meal and fun, someone might notice that the tide was coming in, and if we didn't hurry, we wouldn't be able to get to the skiff. We never became marooned, but we did have wet feet many times. The people in the inner harbor could hear us singing and laughing all the way back.

We have all grown old and do not have a skiff. The flounders have disappeared from the harbor and Sherman's Point is now all private property. Something that cannot be taken away are the memories of good times and great friends. All that enjoyment did not cost one cent.

Manufacturing in Camden for Vessels

S hortly after the Civil War, the Maine coast began building wooden vessels with more capacity and durability than the clipper ships. Camden had some shipyards with records and reputations that certainly became very well known along the East Coast. Many people think we built due to the availability of lumber, but should you peruse pictures of the late nineteenth and early twentieth centuries, you will see that Camden appears to be quite barren.

White pine had been depleted and Maine oak was scarce. Labor did not cost much, as workmen did not mind working long days for little money, and their quality of workmanship was second to none.

Conveniently, the machinery and other important parts for the gigantic wooden vessels came from businesses in town. A major supplier, David Knowlton & Sons, manufactured just about anything needed. The firm also shipped to many other builders, and paid the highest property tax in Camden. It maintained a reputation for quality goods in the industrial world.

David Knowlton had what is known as "Yankee ingenuity," and he moved to Camden from Liberty, Maine, in 1853. In 1880, his four sons joined the firm: A.J.Q., John D., E. Frank and Willis D. Knowlton. At that time the name changed to Knowlton Brothers.

Their foundry made blocks for the first four-masted, five-masted, six-masted and for the only seven-masted vessel ever built. East of Boston, Camden had the only block mill. From the nest of Knowlton's many buildings came power capstans, portable cargo winches, windlasses, ship head pumps, steering wheels, blocks, derricks, deadeyes, brass and iron castings.

At one time, the foundry spread out over four acres and employed one hundred workers. In 1893, they received an order for one hundred thousand trunnel wedges to be used in shipbuilding at Port Blakely, Washington.

This is how Knowlton Brothers Foundry looked in 1883.

David went into business with Haratio Alden, inventing machinery for their oakum factory. With David's invention, they could produce sixty tons of oakum per year.

Another business, the Camden Anchor Works, financed by Mr. Alden and his two sons H.E. and William G. Alden, became the largest anchor manufacturing company in this country. Their anchors sailed all over the world.

In 1894, a New York dealer reported the following to a reporter:

> *The little town of Camden ought to have its name changed to Hope, for it turns out more emblems of hope than all the other places in this country combined. All the stately ships that come out of Maine shipyards look to the village on Penobscot Bay for their anchors. Sturdy smiths swing their hammers day after day, all year long, in the black smoky, long-low-Camden shops, where only anchors are forged. Sometimes the triphammers are going all night about the forges, and the blazing of the fires and ring of the hammers may be seen and heard for miles across the bay. Thousands of tons of old iron are purchased by these establishments every year, for anchors are forged largely from cast-off iron. Anchors of all sizes and weights are turned out from the noisy shops of Camden, the graceful little pleasure boat anchor weighing but a few pounds, as well as the great 5000 pound anchors of the biggest ships.*

Crew is working at Camden Anchor Works.

In 1894, an article in the *Camden Herald* read:

> *An historic anchor belonged to the Frigate* Cumberland, *when the* Merrimac *sank her. In the picturesque little seaport town of Camden, Maine, between Mt. Megunticook's foot and Penobscot Bay, there are two establishments, which share much of the attention of the tourists from the great cities, whose cottages are ranged along the sands of the small islegirt harbor.*
>
> *This is the anchor factory, conspicuous because it is the only place in the country where anchors are made, and a car factory, remarkable because there are no railroads within miles of Camden. The workmen of the Camden anchor forge will tell you of the anchors for famous ships that are hammered out there—anchors that were part of catheads of ocean monarchs of the merchant service and rulers of the wave ships of war.*
>
> *They like to tell how the great mud hook of the gallant frigate* Cumberland *sank in that never-to-be-forgotten battle ram* Merrimac *off Old Point Comfort, came to see the Camden forges. Some years ago the proprietor of the Camden Anchor Works was in Boston. Walking in that part of the city where such thing abound, he examined a lot of wreckage in front of a junk shop, among which was a tremendous anchor, its weight at least three tons. He knew the man that owned the stuff.*
>
> *It had been raised from the wreck of the* Cumberland. *There was no demand for such big anchors, and the anchor-maker made a small offer and*

accepted for the relic. He had it shipped to Camden, where he intended to break it up into old iron. It happened that the owner of a ship, approaching completion at the dock in Rockport came to Camden to order an anchor for his vessel the very day the big mud hook of the historic frigate arrived there. The shipmaster bought it on sight for a good round price.

It was dressed up and fitted with a new stock, and has hung from the bows and held the Maine merchantmen in the harbor in every known sea from that day. The old wooden stock of the Cumberland's *anchor, or what little relic hunters have left of it, is now in the office of the Camden Anchor Works.*

In 1901, Camden Anchor Works was sold to a new corporation, the Camden Anchor-Rockland Machine Company, which manufactured the well-known Knox Gasoline engine.

Amasa Gould Plug and Wedge Mill also did a great business at that time. In 1855, David Knowlton invented a machine for that mill that would manufacture fifteen thousand plugs per day.

Knowlton Bros. had several fires over the years, but the only remaining building has been renovated by Goodwin and became, for a short while, a branch of Eastman Kodak Company. It has been renovated again by MBNA, while they were in town. After being vacant several years, the Camden Anchor Works burned in 1935. Part of that land is the Camden Public Landing.

The great wooden shipbuilding is nearly a thing of the past, with its launchings of many majestic, beautiful and graceful vessels sliding down the ways.

This is the last remaining building of Knowlton Brothers, preserved for business.

John B. Prescott, with Five Masts

When shipyards constructed coastal schooners for the coal trade and for transporting other goods, people had the same vision as today: "bigger is better." That is not always the case, and wasn't back when.

In the mid-1800s, schooners with two masts were everywhere. Then builders began adding another mast, making three in all. Someone thought with four masts they could do better, so yards began constructing them in that manner. If they worked better, why not put five sticks in them? Certainly they would hold more cargo, but five-masters didn't work out as well as anticipated.

Only fifty-eight of the five-masters were ever built. They constructed the first one in Waldoboro, called the *Governor Ames*. The second, *Nathanuel T. Palmer*, was built in Bath. Then Camden, Maine, followed with the third five-master, named the *John B. Prescott*, launched January 13, 1899. In fact, according to Applebee, the latter two were on the stocks at the same time and raced to be the second one. *Palmer* received her document on December 30, 1898, while *Prescott* did not receive hers until January 14, 1899.

At that time, the vessel built in Camden laid claim to being the largest schooner in the world. At eleven o'clock on January 13, 1899, ten thousand people looked on as she slid down the ways at the H.M. Bean yard. It started very slowly because of the cold weather and the weight of the vessel, but then gracefully picked up speed and went into the water. Its graceful lines really made it quite a handsome and spectacular vessel, everyone said.

Holly Bean, the builder, and Captain Crowley, for whom it was built, didn't approve of liquor. So Fannie Prescott christened it with flowers instead of champagne. Fannie's father had the most shares in the vessel, and it had been named for him.

In spite of the cold January weather, a large crowd came from all around, by horse and buggy with the jingle of bells. The trolley cars were also filled

John B. Prescott was the first five-master, built by H.M. Bean.

John B. Prescott, with Five Masts

A crew is caulking the vessel *John B. Prescott.*

This picture shows the humble office of H.M. Bean.

and running, but some did not reach Camden in time for the launching. Some people arrived from Massachusetts by an excursion boat.

The *John B. Prescott* had been described in the *Camden Herald* as follows:

> *The figures of her dimensions are as follows: Length of keel 282 feet, depth 21 feet and width 44 1/3 feet, length of deck from taffrail to forward side bow chock 320 feet, length overall from jigger boom to end of jib boom 410 feet.*
>
> *The five masts are of Oregon pine 112½ feet in length, topmasts 56 feet long making the full height of her masts about 168½ feet. The jigger boom is 77 feet long. The frame is of white oak and cut in Virginia by C.W. Bisbee of Camden. The ceiling and planking are hard pine furnished by Wm. Hasken & Son of Boston and brought here from Georgia.*
>
> *There are four houses on deck, forward house containing engine room and apartments for crew, midship house for the cook, after house containing cabin and apartments for captain and mates and wheel house to protect the man at the wheel.*
>
> *The cabin is finished in fine style and has every convenience. The wood used in the finish are ash, mahogany, cypress and sycamore. Furnishings*

Look at Holly M. Bean, owner the finest vessel building yard on the East Coast.

for the cabin are in keeping with everything about the vessel, and are in the best of style.

Morse & Co., of Bangor furnished the wood for the cabin and Curtis & Spear of Camden the furniture.

The vessel has two decks and a poop deck running to within one berth of the forward hatch. The deck is for protection from the seas and is made very strong, laid with white pine four inches square furnished by Stearns Lumber Co., of Bangor.

The steam engine is 20-horse power and will do all the hoisting of sails, anchors, etc. The vessel will also be heated by steam. J.B. Gifford & Co., of Fall River furnished the sails and Albert Windom & Co., of Boston the rigging.

Her anchors were made in Camden at W.G. Alden's anchor factory and weigh 6000 lbs each. The oakum used for caulking also was made here in Camden from the oakum mill of H.L. Alden. The blocks, castings, etc., were furnished by Knowlton Brothers of Camden. The shieves were furnished by the Duplex Roller Bushing Co., of Camden. The plumbing and furnishings were done by Joseph Bowers and the hardware supplied by J.C. Curtis [both of Camden].

The *John B. Prescott* carried 4,300 tons of coal. They sheathed the vessel with iron to protect her from the ice. The master builder, and also the designer, was a Camden man named J.J. Wardwell. Master joiner for this vessel was H.C. Small; master blacksmith, George D. Sides; master painter, John A. McKay; master caulker, H.C. Buchanan; and spar maker, James Moore. The small boats and carving were done by H.M. Prince.

Holly M. Bean had already built sixty vessels before this one. He began forty-two years before and held a record of building the second three-master ever built, the second four-master and now the third five-master. To top it off, in August of 1900, he launched the first six-master ever built in the world, the *George W. Wells.*

The *John B. Prescott* cost about $83,000.

Mountain View Cemetery

We shall make this history article a little light. People ask me why the people who are six feet under would care about a "mountain view." I really do not have an answer to that one. Another question is, "How many dead people are buried at Mountain View Cemetery," and the only answer I can find is, "All of them."

Many of the people who formed Camden's history are buried here. The first settler, James Richards, and some near relatives had a resting place on their property on Pearl Street. When a descendant in later years built his home on the spot, he had them removed to Mountain View Cemetery. For some reason, I went looking for perhaps a fieldstone, but instead found a nice monument and stone rail around the stones.

The first white male child to be interred is also buried in another part of the cemetery, near the Thorndikes. I believe engraved in stone is "the first white male child born in Camden," meaning the Native Americans were here first. Lewis Ogier, first settler and Revolutionary War veteran, is also buried here.

I enjoy walking in Mountain View Cemetery and speaking to the many people I used to know, or have known through history. A friend of mine is kind enough to plant flowers on the Revolutionary War veterans' graves and also honor them with a Betsy Ross flag.

I often pass the grave of a gentleman who was a well-known Camden photographer. I ask if he remembers when I was only ten years of age and my landlady took me when needed to be the fourth in their whist games. In fact he died while playing whist; so at least he died happy.

There are only two tombs where one can look in, viewing pictures and the two drawers holding the remains. One is Montgomery and the other Grinnell.

Camden built a building near the cannons to be a chapel. It is a lovely little building, but now holds lawn mowers and other maintenance supplies.

The Mountain View Cemetery is a nice place to walk.

The epitaphs always fascinated me. There are some in Mountain View Cemetery that are quite thoughtful. But one epitaph appeared in a newspaper and sparked some trouble. A lady was buried in Sleepy Hollow Cemetery in Concord, Massachusetts, along with such well-known people as Nathaniel Hawthorne, Louisa May Alcott, Ralph Waldo Emerson and Henry David Thoreau.

On her stone, she had engraved, "Who the Hell Is Sheila Shea." Another lady saw that and bought the plot next to it, so on her gravestone she had inscribed, "Damned if I know." Now all the gravestones and inscriptions must have the blessing of the cemetery officials.

Due to my curious mind, I sent for a book of epitaphs in other places through interlibrary loan. I couldn't believe that some people "cast in stone" some things that I wouldn't say, even if I thought them.

To lighten history a little, here are some:

> *THIS SPOT'S THE SWEETEST*
> *I'VE SEEN IN MY LIFE*
> *FOR IT RAISES THE FLOWERS*
> *AND COVERS MY WIFE.*

Lewis Ogier, a Revolutionary War soldier, was one of Camden's first settlers.

How about:

> *To the Memory of*
> *Abraham Beaulieu*
> *Accidentally Shot*
> *April 1844*
> *As a Mark of Affection*
> *From His Brother*

Or:

> *Here Lies Peco Bill*
> *He Always Lied*
> *And Always Will.*
> *Once He Lied Loud*
> *Now He Lies Still.*

A lawyer named John Strange had his read:

> *Here Lies an Honest Lawyer*
> *....................*
> *That's Strange*

> *Sacred to the Memory*
> *Of Anthony Drake,*
> *Who Died for Peace*
> *And Dear Quietness Sake.*
> *His Wife Was Forever*
> *Scoldin and Scoffin*
> *So He Sought Repose*
> *In a $12 Coffin*

> *Jonathan Grober*
> *Died Dead Sober*
> *Lord Thy Wonders*
> *Never Cease*

> *Owen Moore*
> *Gone Away*
> *Owing More*
> *Than He Could Pay*

Here Lies My Wife
In Earthly Mound
Who When She Lived
Did Not But Scold
Good Friends Go Softly
In Your Walking
Should She Awake
And Rise Up Talking

Here Lies a Father of Twenty-nine
There Would Have Been More
But He Didn't Have Time

She Lived With
Her Husband
Fifty Years
And Died in The
Confident Hope
Of Better Life

Another simply read:

He Called
Bill Smith
A Liar

Open, Open Wide
Ye Golden Gates that Lead
To the Heavenly Shore.
Even Father Suffered
Passing Through
And Mother
Weighs Much More.

My Wife Is Dead
And Here She Lies
Nobody Laughs
Nobody Cries
And Where She Is Gone To
And How She Fares

*Nobody Knows
And Nobody Cares*

*Tears Cannot Restore Her,
Therefore I Weep.*

*Sacred to the Memory
Of Jared Bates
His Widow Aged 24
Lives at 7 Elm Street
Has Every Qualification
For a Good Wife
And Yearns
To Be Comforted*

*Beneath These Stones
Lie Back to Back
My Wife and I
When the Last Loud Trumpet
Shall Blow
If She Gets Up
I'll Just Lie Low.*

*Beneath This Stone
A Lump of Clay
Lies Uncle Peter Daniels
Too Early in the Month of May
He Took Off
His Winter Flannels*

And just one more:

Told You I Was Sick.

The book, called *Quaint Epitaphs*, came from the Smithsonian and had to be read in the library and insured for returning. I don't know of any other book like that has been written. We wouldn't have epitaphs like these today…or would we?

"Renascence"

A ssuming that you read about Camden's poet laureate, Edna St. Vincent Millay, your know that her poem "Renascence" is the one that brought her to fame. In fact, it twice changed the course of her life and career. All the time she spent in writing the poem really paid off. It begins:

> *All I could see from where I stood*
> *Was three long mountains and a wood;*
> *I turned and looked another way,*
> *And saw three islands in a bay.*

The poem is very deep to have been written by a teenage girl, and it really has to be studied to understand the feelings that she expressed through the poem. I suggest that although you have probably read it many times, you read it again, trying to think as she did. The full poem appears in the book *Collected Poems Edna St. Vincent Millay.*

The first four lines above are easy for us to understand because we know that she climbed Mount Battie in Camden many, many times. She is definitely describing her favorite view, turning around and then back to where she began. As she continues, even though she loved the place, those were her boundaries. She somehow felt that if she reached high enough, she could touch the sky.

"Renascence" is a metaphor, and this is the first step of the mystic ladder. Infinity settled over her, and she could feel "the ticking of Eternity." In the second step, Vincent is building up emotions, which was easily done, as she could change emotions very quickly. As shown in that poem, she felt that all sinning and atoning was hers. She carried the weight of all the greed and lust in the world.

She then felt fierce fire and perished with them, and also mourned for all. She saw the eyes of the starving man in Capri and knew his hunger, as if it were she. She imagined ships that sank and heard the screams. But then she did not hurt and did not die. When infinity pressed down on her, she suffered death but could not die.

In step three of this mystic ladder of her poem, she was sinking in the ground, six feet under, but then no farther. She felt the weight lift and was gladly dead.

In step four, her mystical vision was the rain that came with a friendly sound. If she were alive again, she would kiss the fingers of the rain. She would miss the blue sky that she would never see, as well as the spring-silver and autumn-gold. She cried to God to give her new birth and bring her back upon the earth. The rains came and struck her grave.

The fifth step is a reflection. She was coming down after "the experience." She sprang up from the grave and laughed at the sky.

It appeared that she now knew God and He could never hide from her. "I know the path that tells Thy way." The world is no wider than the heart; the sky is no higher than the soul is high; "the soul can split the sky in two and let the face of God shine through." Out of the depths of despair, she knew there is always hope.

She ends the poem by writing that if one's soul is flat, the sky will cave in on him, as it did in her "experience."

It is a deep and moving poem when you really think about it as you read. Some of you may translate it differently. Today, it is for many people their favorite poem.

The Whitehall Inn is where "Vincent" read her poem "Renascence," which led her to college.

Mount Battie House

In 1897, Columbus Buswell built a toll road from the old Fay house off Mountain Street to the summit of Mount Battie. In consideration of forty dollars, the performance of certain other agreements and payment of diverse sums of money from time to time, J.H. Fay, Elizabeth Fay and Adeline Harris conveyed to Buswell the exclusive right to charging for travel across their land for ten years.

The grantors had the right to free use of the road and received 15 percent of the income collected from the tolls. Buswell had leased one square acre on top of the mountain from the Adams family. He had the privilege to purchase the land, should they decide to sell it. The same year, Buswell built the Summit House.

Two years later, the Mount Battie Association was formed, principally by summer residents, to hold and protect the mountain as a park. Thousands have enjoyed Mount Battie, with its breathtaking view, thanks to their vision.

The association formed a corporation, purchasing fifty-nine acres that included the top of Mount Battie and the toll road. Local architect W.E. Swartz had designed a building, but when the corporation found they could also purchase the Summit House, they decided to remodel that. The name was changed and it was opened to the public during the summer.

The *Camden Herald* of August 17, 1900, stated the following about the public reception held at the newly remodeled Mount Battie Club House:

> *While people almost everywhere were sweltering in the intense heat Saturday afternoon, those who were on the summit of Mt. Battie were comfortable and cool in the refreshing breeze that Battie always furnishes on a day that is sultry at the base.*

A glass of water at this Mount Battie House cost five cents.

But there were other attractions on Mt. Battie on Saturday afternoon, for members of the Mt. Battie Association were receiving friends and they made that reception a pleasure indeed for their guests.

The Club House just remodeled was thrown open. In the house and on the broad veranda, fair ladies devoted themselves to the pleasure of the visitors.

Meservey's Orchestra of Rockland provided music during the afternoon. The deft hands of the ladies had beautified the interior of the house by decorations of flowers, green boughs and flags.

Light refreshments were also served. More than 100 guests enjoyed the hospitalities offered. The buckboards and public carriages were kept busy transporting the people up and down, and there would have been more guests had the extreme heat not deterred them.

The affair was a great success and a notable event for the town of Camden. Most of the guests saw the remodeled club for the first time, and the transformation from its former plainness was a revelation to them.

The first thing noticed was the picturesque manner in which the dissimilar elements of the former structure had been grouped and combined, making a blending of the old and the new, which was very effective.

The architectural scheme involved first building the large terrace, with walls of mountain stone, extending entirely around the building and permitting a continuous piazza. The fronts and ends of this terrace were finished with curved stone parapets, or bays, giving a castellated effect to the foundation.

From the broad terrace rise the group of club buildings consisting of a picturesque Italian tower and two connecting buildings. The tower has three stories, the upper ones being open galleries commanding the entire mountain view.

Mr. G.D. Spaulding, the popular manager for the past two seasons, was the steward of the house and was assisted by Mrs. Spaulding, a competent cook, waitress, and a stable man, thus guaranteeing the best of service.

There were eight chambers including those necessarily occupied by the help. A dozen guests can easily be accommodated overnight. These rooms are open to the public when not engaged by the club members.

The beds were brass and white enamel with the finest hair mattresses, blankets and bedding, ensuring the comfort of those fortunate enough to spend the night on Mt. Battie.

At 7 p.m., a large company of young people came up for a dance; the association had placed the house at their disposal. A supper was served and many of the afternoon guests remained over to watch the dances and enjoy the music and moon light.

At a reasonable hour, the young people and their chaperones started down the mountain in buckboards and private carriages, terminating what all pronounced one of the most pleasant social events in Camden's history.

It is interesting to note that house rates were $2.50 per day, dinner cost $0.75, supper cost $0.50, breakfast cost $0.50 and lodging was $1.00.

In 1920, the Mount Battie Club House was torn down because, according to the owners, it was not profitable. The present World War I Memorial Tower was built on the spot from some of the mountain stones.

If by chance you have not driven to the top of Mount Battie on the road built in 1965 from Route 1, do it today. The road, owned by the State of Maine Parks Service, is closed in the winter.

The Four-Master
Frederick Billings

For those of us living in the twenty-first century, it is difficult to imagine that Camden and Rockport constructed so many very large vessels over one hundred years ago. On August 11, 1885, Carlton, Norwood & Company (in what is Rockport today) launched the largest American ship of her day, *Frederick Billings*.

This enterprising company, also in the longtime lime industry, built many vessels owned primarily by themselves. Many considered John Pascal, their master builder, one of the finest in Maine. They built schooners and brigs, with each vessel being larger than the one before. The company began the vessel building for the use in lime shipment. Theses vessels, known at that time as "Down Easters," came from the state of Maine. They compared in size with the California clippers of the 1850s, built for the "gold rush." However, the Maine versions were built stronger, so they had the capability of being fast like the clippers, but could also carry large amounts of cargo.

During that time, a depression in shipping came along. In spite of this setback in the industry, Carlton, Norwood & Company decided to build *Frederick Billings*, a four-master. The oak frame had been ordered from Virginia and was delivered in Rockport in May of 1884.

Even after receiving the oak for framing, the company had to make an important decision: whether they should take a chance and build. In October they laid the 263-foot keel for the largest ship ever built on this continent (except for one, the *Great Republic*, built thirty years previously).

In terms of weather, it happened to be a bad winter. But by early spring, hard pine for the planking and ceiling had arrived from South Carolina. Carlton, Norwood & Company hired one hundred men to work on the vessel.

Frederick Billings was being launched in Rockport Harbor.

As it progressed, news spread of the boat of tremendous size. It was said that if one person stood under the bowsprit and looked up at the bow, they looked up 60 feet. She was 290 feet in length.

Pascal's crew had her planked in by June, and the next step took two caulkers. They drove three seams of oakum around her in a workday, to make sure the seams were tight.

The four masts of Oregon pine were towed from Boston by water, and it took several yoke of oxen to pull them out. If you wonder why, the masts measured ninety feet in length and forty-six inches in diameter. Some might refer to them as "big sticks." Henry Bohndell's rigging crew stepped the masts in July, after the spar maker had finished his job.

People around here heard rumors that the vessel would be named *Grover Cleveland*, because it happened to be the largest ship in the country and he was the largest man. But as you know, rumors are not always true. There was a lawyer living in Vermont named Frederick Billings, who had made more money in his practice than the forty-niners did in mining gold. He purchased four sixty-fourths of the vessel for $8,750. In those days, money in vessels were in sixty-fourths, and usually the owner with the largest share could name the vessel for himself, his wife, daughter, girlfriend or anyone else.

I have a copy of a letter from Betty Bates of Rockport written by her grandmother. She said that her dad, Captain Staples, owned the command part of the *Adolph Obrig* and the *Robert Belknap* and a small share in the *Frederick Billings*.

Captain Staples happened to be at sea when they towed the *Frederick Billings* to New York on September 15. Captain Isaac Sherman of Islesboro (later Camden) bought the master's interest of four sixty-fourths, and sailed her on her maiden voyage. The vessel loaded in New York with kerosene for Yokohama.

On her first voyage, the *Frederick Billings* met with easterly gales and had bad weather on most of the first part of her twenty-thousand-mile trip. Being an excellent captain, Sherman made the rough voyage. He made several other trips commanding the Rockport-built vessel. On his last trip, lasting from October 2, 1889, until July 2, 1890, Sherman said it was the worst trip he had ever had, because of weather and rough seas. He then sold his master's interest and retired to Camden.

Captain Herbert Williams of Thomaston took command of the *Billings*. He carried the usual cargo to San Francisco, grain to Le Havre and back to New York that first year. But when the vessel arrived in New York, three of her sailors were put in irons because of mutinous conduct. It is claimed what they did happened while the vessel was being towed from Le Havre to sea. They tried to cut the towing hawser (rope), which could have been the end of the vessel. They also tried to throw the boatswain overboard. When these mutinous men appeared with knives drawn, Captain Williams said he would blow their brains out if they went on the quarterdeck. As they continued to have trouble, the captain had seven of the crew tied up for nine hours with their feet barely touching the deck.

On the next trip from New York to San Francisco, a squall struck and the jibboom broke off. Then the foremast broke off and caused mass confusion on deck, with such a mess of sails and rigging that five of the crew were never seen again. The seas were too rough to try to search for them. The captain decided to clean it up, make the repairs and carry on, even though he was short on crew. Then off Cape Horn another man fell from aloft and died. But *Frederick Billings* finally arrived at San Francisco.

The captain stayed ashore to rest up a while, and joined the *Frederick Billings* again in April. On May 10, 1893, the vessel went to Chile for a load of nitrate. They delivered the heavy cargo, but it had to be stacked and locked so it wouldn't shift in rough seas. The boat carried thirty-nine hundred tons of it. By that evening the crew secured the hatches, ready to sail the next morning.

However, the captain heard someone yell, "Fire!" Smoke poured out everywhere. He managed to get the chief officer's wife out, along with

One looking north in 1881 would get this view of Rockport Harbor.

himself and four men. The nitrate blew the hatches and pieces of wood went two hundred feet into the air. The vessel became a mass of flames. Within seven minutes, another explosion occurred, blowing out the sides and bottom of the vessel. There was very little left of *Frederick Billings* except a few charred timbers.

No one was lost, but there are still questions about the incident. Nitrate doesn't usually cause spontaneous combustion, but once ignited it explodes. It is believed that some of the troublesome crew had tired of working so hard for Captain Williams.

The investors had received only part of their investment in the eight years the ship operated. But the firm of Carlton, Norwood & Company, which had the largest interest, was not insured.

A lovely large painting of the *Frederick Billings* hangs over the fireplace in the Camden Public Library reading room. It depicts the beautiful vessel on very rough seas.

Norumbega

One of Camden's favorite inns, located nearly a mile from town on High Street, is the Norumbega. Many refer to it as "the castle," but there is also a legend about the Land of Norumbega.

About the only thing the cartographers in those very early days seemed to agree upon was that the place *did* exist. Some of them located it extending as far as Florida, but most of the maps placed it in the region of Penobscot Bay—our territory. Gastaldi showed the river of Norumbega in his 1553 map on what is now the Penobscot River. One of the legends also has it to be the site of Bashaba, chief of the Penobscot tribe of Native Americans.

The original legend is attributed to David Ingram of Barking, England. He shipped from Europe with Sir John Lawkins, noted for being one of the most notorious slave traders of his time. The Native Americans turned on them in this country, and they all died, except for young David. It is said that he journeyed far by foot, and was finally picked up off the Maine coast by a European fishing vessel.

In Europe, he spread the story about the Land of Norumbega, where the streets were paved with gold. He stated that rubies, emeralds and diamonds were so plentiful that anyone could help themselves. The women who inhabited this place dressed in soft animal skins, had gold in their ears and were most beautiful. One could have any of these beautiful women, if he would settle down with her. Their large homes had roofs made of gold.

Ingram claimed to have lived with these people, and to be better than they with a bow and arrow. The Bashaba himself wore a diamond in his headdress larger than anyone's fist, as well as a fishnet over him with a pearl in every knot. Ingram claimed he himself ate salmon and venison from a gold platter.

There is no doubt, from David Ingram's description, that he had met with the Native Americans and knew their dress, except for the gold earrings.

They call Norumbega the "castle."

Also there is no doubt that he had seen the fertile fishing grounds of our coast, but he certainly had not seen the large homes with golden roofs.

David Ingram was known in Europe for consuming many tankards in taverns before expounding on the Norumbega in the Penobscot Bay region.

Sir Humphrey Gilbert believed him and left for the fabulous city, even though his vessel needed repairs. Shortly thereafter, he lost his life at sea. Explorer after explorer came searching, without success, until Samuel Champlain explored the area very thoroughly and dispelled the myth.

We might wish that this were all true and we had been living in the middle of it. But Camden has many jewels, perhaps of a different type. Our mountains meet the sea, and in addition we have the beautiful lakes, rivers and ponds. Our town is nearly a perfect place in which to live, and it is filled with people who are real "jewels."

The "castle" Norumbega was built by Joseph B. Stearns 1866, but it is not known for certain that he named it for the area. Mr. Stearns came from a working family, but at age eighteen he became very interested in telegraphy. He moved several times to various states in order to advance in his job. Once he worked in Boston in a fire telegraph office. It was during his time at that job that he gave vital information to President Abraham Lincoln that prevented the Confederates from occupying Arlington Heights, thus saving Washington.

In 1867, Stearns presented his invention to the world—the duplex system of telegraphy. This he patented, selling the rights in the United States and Canada to Western Union. Soon he traveled to England, France and Italy, selling them royalties that made him a very wealthy man.

Although he traveled the world over, he considered Camden to be the most beautiful place of any. Joseph Stearns purchased a tract of land (twenty-three acres with nine hundred feet of shore frontage) on the Belfast Road, and built the magnificent Norumbega from his own design.

The heavy and asymmetrical building constructed by George Glover and D.A. Worthington took six years to complete. On one side there is a heavy porte-cochere and on the other a turret that runs from ground to roof, wide enough for bay windows. The main entrance has stained-glass windows, and the first floor is finished in golden oak paneling.

Stearns kept his rock collection on shelves over the porte-cochere. In the attic he made a darkroom for photography. The home has nine master bedrooms, a library, living room, dining room, a large butler's pantry and a kitchen. He enjoyed all this until his death on July 4, 1895.

On June 1, 1904, Chauncey Keep and Mrs. G.B. Phelps bought the home. It included a stone house, a stable, twenty-five acres, "Roselands Cottage" and one other small cottage on the shore. Mrs. E. Kent Hubbard used it for a summer home during World War I until the late 1930s. Mr. and Mrs. Earl Pitman made it their home for a number of years.

Later Hodding Carter III, press secretary to the secretary of state, bought the castle and referred to it as his "rock pile." In 1984, Mark Borland made the necessary restoration for it to be a bed-and-breakfast.

Murray Keatinge became the second bed-and-breakfast owner in 1987, when it was opened more freely to the public. The guest rooms are lovely. There are four fireplaces on the first floor and four more on the second floor.

The building now serves as an inn. It has seven lovely water-view or mountain-view bedrooms, each with period furniture and private bath. The third floor has a suite overlooking Penobscot Bay. Part of the basement has been finished off as a game room, with a pool table and other sources of entertainment.

In 1993–94, the castle underwent major surgery. Water had seeped through the old mortar and loosened some of the rock walls. A restoration was necessary and was very expensive.

Norumbega is listed on the National Register of Historic Places, and probably is the most photographed building in Camden.

Star Light, Star Bright

Camden has a star that does not appear in the heavens anywhere else in the world. It appears shining brightly each year on Thanksgiving, and remains until the New Year arrives. For miles around, people who do not know its history get very curious about Camden's star.

By talking with locals involved in the project, I learned the following information. The phenomenon began about thirty-some years ago, when a group of merchants in town got together to talk about decorating Camden for Christmas.

At first Bill Brawn placed a wooden star on the outside of French and Brawn, facing Mechanic Street. The merchants placed lights across the streets and the Rotary put Christmas trees on the Village Green. I think that was also about the time the Camden Health Care Auxiliary began to make, decorate and sell wreaths for benefit of the CHCA.

As the group of merchants gathered one day to make plans, someone said, "I wonder how the star on French and Brawns would look up on Mount Battie." They took it up, but it appeared diminished in size somewhat from the mountaintop.

In the December 8, 1966 issue of the *Camden Herald*, the front page shows a picture of the "Christmas Star" as it first appeared. At that time, it measured twelve feet in height, and it burned one hundred electric bulbs of twenty-five watts each.

John Bullard loaned the five-hundred-pound generator that kept the lights going for five hours. Our Camden Hills park ranger, Joseph Fortier, went up each evening to fill it with gasoline.

The first Sunday evening that the star shone down on Camden, many citizens were concerned "about the strange glow" on Mount Battie. Some thought it to be a fire burning (thinking back to days long ago when we did have a very serious fire on the mountain that burned for days before it could be contained). Others felt sure it must be a flying saucer. Both the police station and the fire station answered many calls that night.

The businessmen who set up the star and pledged its upkeep were Wilfred Michaud, Robert Barron, Leroy Morong, Carl Cornish, James Callahan and Rodney Boynton. The Lions soon took over the project of a star on Mount Battie, and they continue to this day to see that it is there for all to enjoy.

Raymond Drinkwater built a larger one of steel with light bulbs in it. Frank Rankin leads a group of about six to eight Lions every year to get the star from the Rankin Hardware Barn in Hope, where it is stored. It takes them about four and a half hours to put it together. Some pieces are very long.

The star hangs from the Memorial Tower. Two-thirds of it is above the tower and about one-third below the tower. In addition it has what I call stanchions that keep it securely in place. The wind can be very powerful up on Mount Battie some evenings.

About five years ago, Bill Glover at his Steel Works built the second metal star. It holds ninety-two bulbs of fifteen watts each, which Frank Rankin has generously supplied for years. Over time, the first star frame became weatherworn and was occasionally vandalized. Someone even stole the generator a few years ago, much like the Grinch who stole Christmas.

Robert Oxton has gone up Mount Battie every night between Thanksgiving and New Year to carry gasoline to the generator for most of the years it has been in operation. We call that sincere community dedication. It takes about three gallons per night, a supply which is now donated by Mr. Fowlie of the Village Variety. Bob fills the generator about 4:00 p.m., and it goes until it runs out of gasoline, sometime after midnight.

The Lions add that to their many projects, as does Archie Bailey, who was one of the merchants who came up with the idea. Frank Rankin, Robert Oxton and others also add that to their many helping projects.

I understand that Oxton took a whole group of Lions to see it firsthand, on top of Mount Battie. Some of the newer members had never seen it close up, even though they support the project. Other people have a tradition to go up to see it lit, and others go up when it is the last night.

A friend of mine who once lived in Rockport would call me each year to say, "I can see your beautiful star from my kitchen window." People in Islesboro and other places also can see it. A youngster visiting my neighbors this past Thanksgiving called her parents to look at a star that she had never seen before. She questioned, "How did it get there?"

A couple of years ago, *Down East Magazine* published an article about it, and a beautiful picture of our "Christmas Star" appeared on the cover of

Camden's Christmas Star shines from Mount Battie. *Courtesy of photographer Mark Wallack.*

that issue. Only a professional photographer could take a good picture of it. But just look out your window when it is up for the Christmas season, or look from some place where you get a view of Mount Battie. It is said that mid–High Street is the best vantage point. It is wonderful to see.

Now you know the secret if you didn't know before. We appreciate the time and effort the Lions and others put into that project for all of us to enjoy.

New Friends Are Silver,
but Old Friends Are Gold

Years ago, or perhaps even eons ago, I attended the seventh grade (now called junior high) in the Brick Building (which was then called the Mary E. Taylor School, but recently had its name changed again). My social studies teacher said we could write to a pen pal in a foreign country. That sounded very exciting, and it didn't take me long to decide to whom I wished to correspond. So I filled out the paper requesting correspondence with a boy in France.

It took a little while, probably weeks that seemed like years, for the whole process to go through. I had almost forgotten about it when I received a letter from Hawaii (not part of the United States then), written by Joan Kaneshiro. Really, at that age, my disappointment seemed insurmountable. I had visions that the French boy would be tall, dark and handsome. But after a quick recovery, I really enjoyed our exchange of letters. Never have I thought to ask her if she had requested a different country or gender than she received.

The Great Depression still encompassed us in the mid-thirties, so most likely we did not have cameras or money to develop film. Without snapshots, we wrote descriptions of our countries, family and friends. She had more brothers and sisters than I, as I had only one of each. Her parents came from Japan and mine came from Islesboro, Maine, and Beirut, Lebanon. School during those years seemed to be our main activity, and we both enjoyed our school years. When it came time to graduate in 1942, we exchanged graduation pictures. Now we each knew what our pen pal looked like, and felt happy that we had a face to go with the letters.

She became my "kanaka" (Hawaiian sister) and I her "haole" (Anglo-Saxon sister). Some people in the United States believed "haole" was a derogatory word, but it is a Hawaiian word originally meaning foreigner, but now used to mean Caucasian.

My Hawaiian pen pal, Joan Kaneshiro, sent me her graduation picture.

Our lives continued very much on the same course, except for our food and the climate. I wrote about below-zero weather and snowstorms, while she had flower gardens all year long. She still thinks it is unbearably cold when it is in the sixties. Below-zero weather is beyond her comprehension. Her weather, living in temperatures ninety or one hundred degrees every day, I could not tolerate. I tell her that we Maine people have ice water in our veins.

After school, we both went to work ("hanahana") in offices. She worked for the government and I for Camden Shipbuilding (now Wayfarer Marine). Once we started working, we had cameras and money to send pictures.

I sent Joan my graduation picture. We then knew what one another looked like.

About twenty years after we became pen pals, we exchanged pictures in our finest attire. We both lived in three-inch heels. I walked one and a half miles to work in them, worked all day, walked home at night and quite often went dancing in the evening. Her dress appeared more conservative than mine. My boss and his wife brought a beautiful red one back to me from Fifth Avenue for a birthday present. It was lined, and probably the most expensive dress I had owned to date. But the only time I wore it was in one snapshot. My then boyfriend thought the "spaghetti straps" were too revealing and wouldn't be seen with me in it. Unbeknownst to my boss and his wife, I gave it away to a friend in the city, where people dressed more liberally than in Camden.

When the phone rings at midnight and I hear "Aloha," I know it is my dear friend Joan calling me, as there is a six-hour time difference. We always remember each other's birthday and Christmas. ("Care packages" arrive in between times.) Priority mail is generally delivered from Honolulu to Camden or vice versa in two days. That is quicker than getting a postcard from Camden to Camden.

We continued to exchange pictures. Mine showed fields, snowstorms and over the years a few flowers, as well as my furry and feathered friends. She sent beautiful pictures of Hawaii, working on her lawn and of her husband. We shared each other's joy and sorrows through the years.

Joan and Howard Moriyama love to travel, and they know I do not. So in 1984 they came to Camden with a niece and nephew, Albert and Lillian. I said I would meet them at the shopping center to lead them to my house. They went right by our designated meeting spot, because what I called a "shopping center" was the Hannaford grocery store and three banks. In Honolulu, a "shopping center" meant something much, much larger. They did turn around and come back, and we finally met for the first time, after almost fifty years of friendship. Upon sight, we both felt a close bond.

After their departure, the phone calls came, saying, "Why don't you come to Honolulu? We would like to spoil you rotten. We know all the places to go, and you stay with us." I would say, "Mahalo (thank you), but aole (no). I do not like to kaahele (travel)." Joan seemed pleased that I used Hawaiian words, even with the Maine accent.

So again in 1987 they made it to Maine. They had picked up Joan's sister Marilyn and friend May in New York. The autumn leaves couldn't have been more beautiful. My visitors had not seen such a change of colors, and wanted to pick up every leaf. I told them they would just dry up and crumble. So I took two pieces of clear plastic and put the various leaves between them, and then pressed it together. The Moriyamas kept it in their home to look at for a long time. They wanted a part of Maine with them at home.

While Honolulu still waited for me, I received macadamia nuts, chocolates, cookies, Hawaiian coffee, figurines and more goodies than I can name. They received Maine blueberry jam, maple sugar candy, maple syrup and Maine cards.

So in 1990 they made the trip again to visit me and their great-niece Emi Moriyama, who then lived in Augusta. Again we enjoyed everything. One night we went to Augusta to visit Emi and there had the Moriyamas' favorite dish: Maine lobsters. Although our visits have been short, they have been filled with fun and enjoyment.

Joan's husband, Howard, has since passed away, but someday she will visit me again.

People seem surprised to hear that I have had a pen pal for seventy years, and our friendship continues to grow. I am happy now that I didn't get the letter from a tall, dark and handsome French boy, as our correspondence probably would not have lasted.

Peter Ott and Son, Peter Oat

Side by side in Camden's Mountain View Cemetery, in section 4 lots 82 and 83, lie Peter Ott and his son, Peter Oat. The father's birth date is May 1733 in Germany, and he died in Camden on December 20, 1824. His son, Peter Oat, was born in about 1760 in Camden and died October 16, 1825, also in Camden.

The name of Ott was taken from the Old German emperor's given name, Otto, made famous by Otto the Great in the tenth century. I believe the spelling perhaps happened because they were of German nationality, and Ott in their language is pronounced sounding like Oat.

In 1732, General Samuel Waldo wanted settlements for the Waldo Patent, so he sent agents to Germany, inducing the emigrants to form a German colony at Broad Bay (Waldoboro). A few years later, he sent his son to entice the people to come here and settle.

From a German newspaper, *Imperial Post*, an article read like this:

> *The climate is acknowledged to be healthy, and the soil is exceedingly fruitful, since the wood that grows there is mostly oak, beech, ash, maple and the like, and it yields all manner of fruit as in Germany, but hemp and flax in greater perfection. Also there is much game in the woods, and many fish in the streams, and everyone is permitted to hunt and fish.*

History has it that the people who made the long voyage over from Europe were not happy about the climate. One of those emigrants happened to be Peter Ott, who left Broad Bay and went to Boston for a time to run a tavern.

He returned to Camden to run a tavern on Lot #20, which is presently on Route 1 in Rockport, where town meetings were held some of the time when the Harbor and Goose River were both Camden. The British raiders or marauders seemed to choose Goose River as a favorite place.

Just look at the vista at Mountain View.

Elizabeth, daughter of Peter Ott, was tending the tavern when a group of British decided to take over. They began to draw liquor from a barrel in the cellar. She followed them down and told them to stop. When they refused, she put her hand over the spout to stop its flow. One raider then placed a gun to her head, but she bravely insisted on protecting her father's property. They left without harming her or the property.

After its incorporation in February 1791, Camden held its first town meeting on April 4, 1791, at Peter Ott's Inn. At that time, Camden consisted of the Harbor (Camden), Goose River (Rockport), Clam Cove (Glen Cove) and West Camden (West Rockport).

According to Locke's *History of Camden 1605–1859*:

> *The officers there chosen were Wm. Gregaory, moderator; John Harkness, town clerk; John Harkness, 1st selectman; Wm. Gregory, 2nd selectman; Wm. McGlathery, 3rd selectman; Paul Thorndike, constable; Nathaniel Palmer, tax collector; Joseph Eaton, treasurer; James Richards, Robt. Thorndike and David Nutt, surveyors of lumber &c. Five men were likewise chosen as Tythingmen: (those persons were a terror to Sabbath breakers), and two to the distinguished office of hog reeves.*

Sometimes after that they held town meetings at Peter Ott's at Goose River, and other times at the Harbor. They seemed to hold meetings in the two sections alternately. The two sections argued at most meetings.

The stone is that of Peter Ott, who owned a tavern.

The stone beside him is his that of his son, whose name was spelled Peter Oat Jr.

Peter Ott and Son, Peter Oat

Peter Ott Sr. and his wife (whose name is unknown) had four children: Peter Jr., who married Beulah Richards Upham; Elizabeth, who married Lieutenant John Harkness; John Jacob, who married Nancy Hopkins of Pownalboro; and Nancy, who married Aaron Rowell of Pownalboro.

Peter Ott Jr. (or Peter Oat) served in the Revolutionary War as a private in Maine, Plummer's Company, for six months, and was a private under General Ulmer for two months and sixteen days.

When his widow was about eighty years of age, she applied for a pension. When I sent for the papers, there were thirty-eight of them. They consisted of letters to prove that Beulah was Peter's wife, and then more letters to prove that the people proving Beulah had to prove themselves. Apparently there always has been a lot of "red tape" concerning government documents. Elizabeth Harkness wrote to prove that Beulah married her brother Peter, and that had to be notarized by a justice of peace. Lewis Ogier stated in a letter that he had been a neighbor and that Peter joined the expedition to Bagaduce. Then a justice of peace had to testify that Lewis Ogier was an outstanding citizen and respectable in every way so that what he had said would be believed.

William Gregory stated that Peter Ott Jr. served in the militia going to Bagaduce (Castine), and also was at Pine Hill (Glen Cove). Then a justice of the peace stated that he knew William Gregory, and what he said was to be believed.

The letters go on and on until finally the pension was "inscribed on a roll" at the rate of $28.44 per annum beginning March 4, 1843. After all of that, I do hope the widow Ott spent it carefully.

Unsolved Murders in Camden

No way!" people say when you tell them that there actually have been people murdered in Camden.

Ada Mill, who was somewhat of a recluse, lived on a large parcel of land on the Hosmer Pond Road. She was a nice old soul who lived in a little shelter alone. The town of Camden wanted some of her property for what is known today as the Oak Hill Cemetery. The town had long-range vision, and knew they would run out of cemetery plots at Mountain View Cemetery. More people were dying than ever before, and Camden needed room for them.

The town manager, Percy Keller, negotiated for quite some time with Ada to sell some of her land to Camden. They both eventually agreed, and I assume that she had been paid the money for the land on July 2, 1936, as they settled the transaction.

Soon after that, on July 11, 1936, the town manager spotted her body during an organizational search. It never became clear just why they had been searching for her. Camden residents all expressed complete surprise and shock to hear that Ada's badly beaten body had been found about four hundred feet from her little shelter, about three days after her murder. Fir boughs partially covered her frail body, and a crowbar found nearby was presumed to be the murder weapon. Her right arm had been broken, and there had been at least four blows to her head.

Many theories circulated around town as to why someone had murdered her. Many thought it happened because of the money she had from the sale of the land. Others said Ada probably had been "done in" by two convicts who had escaped from the Maine State Prison in Thomaston. She would not have been any match for the two men. If so, why didn't they just take her money and leave her alive?

The county sheriff, Earle C. Ludwig, offered a $1,000 reward from the state attorney's office, hoping that would solve the murder. A prominent summer resident stated that if authorities were unable to solve the murder of the eighty-six-year-old woman, then he would move away. They couldn't, and he did.

On April 25, 1940, Mrs. Benjamin Morong, walking Union Street, spotted a nude infant in the Jacob's Quarry. She notified the Camden Fire Department, which quickly arrived on the scene and removed the tiny body. It was taken to Good's Funeral Home and Dr. Weisman and Dr. Hutchins performed an autopsy. But the body, by the time it was found, had decomposed and they came up with only the answers that the boy had been about five months old and he was dead before someone threw him in the quarry.

Authorities checked birth records in this area for the past year, but came up with no information. A $500 reward had been offered, but that crime is still unsolved. The *Camden Herald* suggested $0.25 donations until $25 had been raised for a marker for the grave. The little body had a burial in the Seaview Cemetery in Rockport with the inscription "Unknown— Unwanted, Baby Boy. Body found in Rockport quarry, April 20, 1940. Age about five months."

Someone placed flowers on the grave for many years. People did not know whether they had been placed by a guilty person or a caring one.

Yes, I have more to tell you about a mystery that occurred on Highland Avenue. In the 1940s, there were no apartment houses for the elderly or any houses on that road, including mine. It had just a dirt road that lead to nowhere except Greenfield, and it was surrounded by woods.

Two hermits each had a little cabin in the woods with a well they shared. One of them, Lawrence Carroll, simply disappeared, never to be found. He had a personality a little different than most of us, but he was smart in many ways. He did some oil painting and also had a rock collection. He rigged up a motor from a vacuum cleaner to polish the rocks. As we lived on Chestnut Street, and it being just a short walk through the woods, my father used to visit them once in a while.

I went with him a couple of times, and Mr. Carroll gave me a small rock collection and told me the name of each rock. I guarded them like diamonds, as I didn't know the names of Jasper stones, quartz, etc., until that visit.

The rumors circulated around town when he disappeared. Some said that he had a small World War I pension that supported him, and maybe someone knew he had some money on a certain day, then robbed and killed him.

The police searched the well and the woods, but found no trace of him. He perhaps had been weighted down and thrown in the quarry. Another

Lawrence Carroll, a World War I veteran, mysteriously disappeared. *Courtesy of Camden American Legion.*

theory, but quite far-fetched, was that the "summer people" had found him another place to live—in another town. However, to this day, there have been no answers to solve his disappearance.

One more unfortunate resident of Camden, Ida Phinney, lived at 5 Willow Street in a large home that her parents had owned before her.

One evening the couple who also lived there came home and her bedroom door was closed as usual, so they did not wake her. But the next morning, on March 17, 1962, when they neither heard nor saw her, they called the police.

They found Phinney's body in the cistern in the cellar, and her glasses rested on top. Dr. David Mann, who was Knox County medical examiner at that time, stated that she had died of cerebral thrombosis before going into the cistern. They found no fingerprints, so that became another Camden unsolved murder.

Rockland had some mysterious murders, and so did Tenants Harbor. It didn't happen just in beautiful Camden, Maine.

Vessel Building in Camden, Maine

In the past, many of Maine's coastal towns built wooden vessels as a major industry. Camden held its place high on the list for nearly two hundred years.

It began on the west side of Camden Harbor, as Captain William McGlathery started it all when he built the twenty-six-ton sloop *Industry* in 1792. Native Americans and some early settlers built boats, but McGlathery's became the first one documented. Peter Ott's Restaurant is now on the site of that yard. The captain went out of business in 1799 and moved to Frankfort, Maine.

Camden did not build Bay View Street until 1866, so the land went from Chestnut Street down to the harbor. It is difficult to imagine no Bay View Street.

In 1800, Noah Brooks arrived in Camden and started a shipyard with Benjamin Cushing. I sense that Noah had the know-how, and Benjamin had the money. They built the vessel *Camden* that same year. During the War of 1812, their yard prominently built and repaired vessels.

Deacon Joseph Stetson came next, and he constructed about seventy vessels in all. His shipyard went from Chestnut Street down to where the Public Landing is today. He had his business from 1819 to 1853, but moved it to the head of the harbor in 1840. I like to give him the title "father of coffee breaks." Up until that time, the workers drank grog (rum and blackstrap molasses). They began their working day with it, and imbibed again mid-morning, with their lunch and in the mid-afternoon, as they worked long days in the cold. When they laid a keel for a new vessel, they also called, "Grog Ho!" as they did when finishing the planking, and always for any launching.

The temperance movement had swept over Camden in 1829, before Neil Dow's law had been enacted, when liquor could be for medicinal purposes only. Deacon Stetson felt it his duty as a Christian, and also for the good of the workmen, to change the grog habit to coffee. But some of the staunch old Mainers did not feel that coffee had much substance. However, they survived the change and the "Old General" (one of his original coffeepots) did as well. It was used for many Camden social functions, and now it is an heirloom of the First Congregational Church.

In 1854, Deacon Stetson sold his yard at the head of the harbor to John Witherspoon, who leased it out to various builders. Later Augustus Myrick bought it.

On the west side of the brook in the 1850s, on land owned by Elijah Grover, Oliver Clarey had a shipyard going that he later purchased. Israel Decrow began building there until Captain Isaac Coomb went into partnership with Decrow. Later in 1871, David Decrow bought the land and subdivided it with Israel Decrow.

John E. Dailey built two vessels in Deacon Stetson's yard in 1862, and then moved to Tenants Harbor. He said he would someday return to Camden to build, which he did. On Camden's map of 1875, it shows the east side of the brook as land belonging to John E. Dailey.

After a successful vessel building career, Dailey died in 1863, and Isaac Coombs began shipbuilding there. He took in different partners, so the company had various names from time to time.

During a fifty-year span, the head of the harbor had many shipyards that constructed vessels, before Atlantic Avenue had been built and land went from High Street to the water. That became the prominent location, with no shipyards left on the west side of the harbor.

Moving down Sea Street to Eaton's Point, Thomas Hodgman and Russell Glover had a yard for a few years around 1855. That yard remained empty until Holly Bean purchased the land in 1875. He became one of the best-known builders in Camden, with seventy-one vessels to his credit, including some outstanding ones. Bean's yard constructed a brig, a couple of barks, a two-master, seventeen three-masters, twenty four-masters, twelve five-masters and one six-master.

On August 14, 1900, the Bean yard launched the first six-master in the world, the *George W. Wells*. It took one year and four months from laying the keel to launching. She slid down the ways with ten thousand people watching the great event of the launching of the largest vessel at that time.

The Percy and Small Yard in Bath, Maine, launched the *Eleanor Percy* just two months after. On June 29, 1901, the only two six-masters in the world collided. Newspapers reported that neither captain nor crew admitted fault. The following Thursday, the *George W. Wells* was towed to the Percy and Small yard for repairs. That answered the question.

Harry Dailey and his father, John, built boats at the "head of the harbor."

Robert Bean built the vessel *Charles Dean*.

Launching of vessels always had beautiful ribbons, as did the *Nellie S. Bean*.

The *George W. Wells* continued as a very fast vessel, and her third captain, Joseph York, enjoyed breaking records with her. He loved that vessel, but little did he realize when he set out for Florida in September of 1913, the vessel would meet her demise. They ran into a storm off North Carolina; the winds blew out her sails and she took a severe pounding. They could not save the vessel, but thanks to Captain York, everyone aboard survived, including two women, two infants, a goat, Fluffy the cat and a dog.

Robert L. Bean had been associated with his father in building, so he had it in his blood. He tried to bring to life the yard after his father closed it, but within two years it closed again. He did not have a crew or anything with which to work, except his sheer determination.

In 1914, Robert Bean went to New York and came back with a contract. Two years later the *Percy Pyne* was launched. There should have been a great celebration, as it was the first vessel launched in seven years. But no colors flew and there was no sign of a christening. Later, a German engine arrived with a man to supervise its installation. *Percy Pyne* became the largest auxiliary-powered schooner built on this coast. Later a German crew arrived. Rumors later had it that the vessel had been built to be a commerce raider.

Robert Bean's yard constructed nine other vessels, with contracts from various places. He held fast to his belief that "wind and water" still had to be the cheapest mode of transportation. Times changed at the end of World War I. The four-master that once sold for about $225,000 could no longer be sold for $500. That placed Mr. Bean in serious financial difficulties, and tall ships were lost to progress.

A group of Penobscot Indians were part of the *Pine Tree I* ceremony.

First Lady Eleanor Roosevelt leaving the luncheon with her hostess, Mrs. Richard Lyman.

Again the Bean Yard stayed silent for twenty years, until World War II broke out. Cary Bok, Richard Lyman and Clinton Lunt (all under age thirty) quickly brought the yard back for the war effort. What a difficult task to build ways and find enough workers and equipment. The yard eventually reached a peak of fifteen hundred employees, working two shifts.

Because the young men had left for war, the yard became so desperate for workers that they placed a full-page ad in the *Camden Herald* offering to hire women. Those hired would have to do a man's work and all glamour would be lost. Lips would lose their allure, and the women would wear mackinaws and boots for warmth.

After building a couple of minesweepers, the shipyard heard that President Franklin D. Roosevelt needed someone to build wooden barges. The president became very concerned about getting coal up here in the winter. The builders of steel crafts didn't want to bother with lowly barges, and no one knew how to build them anyway.

Camden Shipbuilding & Marine Railways wanted that contract. They learned that after the Civil War, the Kelley and Spear Yard had built some wooden barges. By searching around for home decorations of half models, an architect drew up plans.

One of the biggest days for Camden, Maine, occurred on February 8, 1943. Mrs. Eleanor Roosevelt (the first lady) came here to christen the first barge launched, *Pine Tree I*. When word got out that the First Lady would be arriving, the chamber of commerce became flooded with calls from the Associated Press, Wide World, International News Service, Fox Movietone, Paramount, Hearst and many others. (Television wasn't yet around.) The shipyard set up a press conference, with Hamilton Hall in charge. Many of the reporters wrote their stories before the event actually took place, confirming details by telephone immediately after.

I don't believe any FBI men came here in those days. Cary Bok picked Mrs. Roosevelt up in Portland, and a select group had lunch with her at the Lyman house at 73 Chestnut Street. The Camden Fire Department, in their dress uniforms, served as police control, as Camden had only one night watchman as their police force. Thousands of people thronged to Sea Street and Chestnut Street. After a successful launching, they held a tea and reception at the Officers' Club at 10 Sea Street.

Reverend Bukelman and his younger daughter walked back from the launching. She cried her little heart out, and an officer on the porch asked, "What is wrong with the little girl?"

Her father told him how disappointed she was not to have seen Mrs. Roosevelt when she launched *Pine Tree I*, because so many people stood in front of her.

The officer on duty took the little girl inside, where Mrs. Roosevelt held her on her lap and gave her milk and cookies. When they arrived back at the Methodist church and the service was about to begin, the little girl ran down the aisle, full of excitement and yelled, "I just sat in the government's lap!"

In three years, the shipyard turned out two minesweepers, eleven APcs, four coal barges, twelve ATRs and received the Army-Navy E Award for efficiency.

After World War II, Cary Bok and William Peterson built fishing boats and private yachts from 1943 to 1963, with Malcolm Brewer as master builder. A few to mention were a forty-two-foot sloop for the Honorable Curtis Bok named *Alphard*, which sailed to England. In 1949, the yard constructed a fifty-five-foot cruiser, *Fantasy*, followed by a seventy-foot luxury cruiser, *Anahita*. What a beautiful handcrafted yacht that was, with pure white silk curtains, red carpeting and all the navigational equipment available at the time. Then they built a forty-foot ketch, designed to go around the world

An ATR is photographed on trials.

with the owner, his wife and crew of two. They named her the *Frances USA*. A total of thirty-two vessels were built at Camden Shipbuilding Co.

Eventually, it became impossible to make a profit on these contracted yachts. Again the yard found itself in financial difficulties, and had to be sold. The new owners discontinued building, keeping the business of a repair, service and storage facility, as it is today as Wayfarer Marine Company.

We are proud of Camden's rich history in building such beautiful wooden vessels for so many years.

A launching party was held for the workmen who built the yacht *Alphard*.

One of the fanciest yachts built by Camden Shipbuilding Co., Inc., was *Anahita*.

Walking Tour of Camden

Let's start at Long's Funeral Home. I don't know about you, but I would rather start there than end there. Did you know it was previously called Good and Laite...or was it Laite and Good? Anyway, it was quite appropriate. The brick structure was built in 1852–53 and was known as the Brick School House. I know that in 1899, the first grade had Miss May Bowers teaching, and the fifth grade had Miss Duplissa. During this time there were other schools in town, with classes at the Elm Street School, the Cleveland Hall, the Cobb School, the Millville School and the Mansfield school. They had one teacher for six grades. There were no buses and no automobiles; everyone walked to school. The Brick School House was leased to the Grange in 1905. The Grangers built their own building later on the south side, which is now a parking lot for the Farmer's Union.

The Farmer's Union used to be the Episcopal church. In 1855, the Universalists used it for a meetinghouse, until the Episcopal parish bought it in 1856. They used it for a number of years. (On the north end is still one of the church windows.) One story tells that while Reverend Hayden was preaching, the roof was leaking and running down the back of his neck. He was about to leave on vacation and made it known that they needed a new church. He was popular, and by the time he returned from vacation, his parishioners had raised money for a new church on Chestnut Street, which was built in 1924.

Across from the Farmer's Union was the Methodist church. The previous one was located behind what is now the Camden Opera House and was destroyed in the Great Fire of Camden. The house on this lot was moved to Sea Street (where it still remains), and the Methodist church was built in 1893–94 for $15,000. Camden and Rockport decided to consolidate and built the St. John Methodist Church on John Street. The closing for this

The Brick School is now Long's Funeral Home.

former church was in April 1988 for one-quarter of a million dollars. It is now four condominiums.

The section known as "Monument Square" for many years was so called because the Soldier's Monument (from the Civil War) was located in the center where the four roads come together. An association was formed to raise the money for a monument. By 1899, after ten years, they had raised $800, and they then accepted donations from the public. A tribute to those who served in Camden in the Civil War was a dream come true. Well, the poor Union soldier began to be hit when cars came into being. In 1968, the last time it was hit, the poor soldier fell from his base, broke both arms and lay in pieces. After some controversy, an extensive repair job was done and he was moved to Harbor Park. He now watches the flow of traffic on busy Main Street.

On the lot where the Camden Public Library stands there once was a hotel, the Ocean House. According to information found, it burned in 1903. Through the generosity of Mary Curtis Louise Bok (later Zimbalist), the lot was purchased for a library. There had been a library from time to time in Camden, but not like this one. A group headed by Mrs. Charles Montgomery began opening its homes for card parties and other events

This Methodist church was turned into condominiums.

It was called Monument Square because the Civil War monument was once located there.

This is the original Camden Public Library, before the underground addition.

to raise money. World War I came along, and that slowed down their efforts. But in 1920, Mrs. E. Kent Hubbard met with the association and they began to raise money once more. Mr. Parker Morse Hooper gave his services, along with Charles Loring of Boston, to be the architects. On June 28, 1928, the Camden Public Library opened its doors. In order to create more space, a new underground Centennial Wing was dedicated on Sunday, September 29, 1996. Mrs. George Bush (first lady) was the keynote speaker. It is a beautiful place used by many, both young and old.

Mrs. Bok also purchased land and donated it for an outdoor amphitheater—designed by Fletcher Steele of Boston—that adjoins the library. In 1930, it was the first public park the noted landscape architect had designed. An independent commission worked several years recently on plans to preserve, renovate and/or restore the amphitheater, library grounds and Harbor Park.

The Great Fire of 1892 was the most disastrous fire that Camden ever had. It started in the Cleveland Block; the water pressure was inadequate, and a fierce easterly wind fanned the flames. Within hours, forty or more buildings were destroyed, including all their contents. In these buildings were sixty businesses, ten societies and eighteen families. In financial terms, they lost $300,000 to $500,000. The businessmen got together and decided to invest in buildings that were safe and also to straighten the streets, while they were about it. It is difficult to believe that just one year later, all the brick buildings you see on Main and Elm Streets today had

The hotel Ocean House was on the location of the present-day Camden Public Library.

been constructed. On Main Street, it starts with the Fletcher Block (the Boynton-McKay Store) and was followed with the Masonic Block (Rockport Blueprint today), the Russell Block, Huse Block, Cleveland Block and on the end the Adams Block. Across Main Street, and also built of brick at that time, are Hodgman, Burd and Arau Blocks. The Travelers' Inn (Allen Agency for many years) was built soon after. Go to town and look up, but don't stand in the middle of the road or you may end up like the Civil War monument, perhaps facing west forever.

As you head up Elm Street, the brick buildings built after the fire were French and Brawn, followed by the Curtis Block. Still headed south up Elm Street are the Curtis, Gill and Bisbee Blocks. The tallest one on the corner of Washington and Elm is the French Block. Across Washington Street is the beautiful Camden Opera House.

When the Opera House was first built after the fire, the Village Corporation asked the legislature if they might raise money to build the Camden Opera House. Some people opposed the new building, saying that maintenance on it would be too much. They petitioned the supreme judicial court for an injunction to stop the construction. Judge Foster of Bath denied the injunction, and the building was completed. The *Camden Herald*

When the Camden Opera House was built, the auditorium looked like this. It was restored a few years ago to look exactly the same.

of April 27, 1894, describes the beautiful building, including the balcony decorated by William Carleton. On June 8, 1894, the grand opening was described. Many different events have been held there over the years, and in 1930 it was changed somewhat. One hundred years later, through more generosity, it was again restored to look exactly as it did when first built. It is beautiful.

The Congregational church has been at its present location since 1834. You know, it is located where the "go through anyway stop sign" is, just above Free Street. The church has been remodeled a couple of times over the years. Its parish house was across the street, where the *Camden Herald* office and another store are today. The new parish was added on the church in 1955. Children no longer had to cross Elm Street to go to Sunday school.

Beside that building is the Elm Street School and the Conway Boulder. Conway was a native who served for forty-five years in the U.S. Navy. In 1861, his commandant (a traitor) agreed to surrender the Pensacola Navy Yard to the Confederates. When the enemy ordered Conway to haul down the flag so the Confederate flag could be raised, he refused. Without hesitation, he turned from the flagstaff and said, "I won't do it, sir; that is the flag of my country. I have served under it many years and won't dishonor it now."

Conway's commanding officer was court-martialed. The secretary of the navy issued a general order to be read at all naval stations telling about it. Forty-one years after Conway's death, Camden decided to honor him with the thirty-ton boulder moved from Ogier Hill (upper Chestnut Street). That day in 1906, Camden celebrated with a large parade and several battleships in our harbor. One hundred years later, Camden celebrated once more.

The Elm Street School has a long history. A small school was near that location in 1794, and part of that school is still in existence on "Turkey Turd" Lane, except today we call it Wood Street. In 1820, a large yellow building made a school on the present location of the Elm Street School. That one was sold, moved and used for a mill and later burned. Then another was built, called "School House Hall," burned in 1868. The following year, the present Elm Street School building was built and was known as the high school until 1904, when they built the Camden High School on Knowlton Street, now demolished.

On the present Village Green, a large hotel (known by several names but most commonly known as the Bay View House), burned November 17, 1917. There were stores on that space, but they were moved in 1928, when the Village Green designed by Olmsted came into being.

The Chestnut Baptist Church has been next door on Chestnut Street since 1837. They rebuilt it in 1868, and a clock was placed in the steeple from contributions and the untiring efforts of David Knowlton. The spire had to be cut down in 1887 because it was considered unsafe. Billy Young, an Eagle Scout, made it his project to have the spire replaced in 1980.

Next to the Baptist church is the Hathaway-Cushing house. Mr. Hathaway was Camden's first lawyer, who married Deborah Cushing. Unfortunately, the lawyer Hathaway died very young.

St. Thomas rectory once was part of the Hathaway-Cushing property built in 1824. The typical English village church, St. Thomas Episcopal is very lovely. That was built in 1924, and the stained-glass windows came from England.

The construction of the Camden Post Office took place in 1914, and it was opened in May of 1915. It was saved by Camden people several years ago, when the government wanted to build a new one in a different location. Camden felt that it was an important place in the middle of town. Perseverance and persistence won over the federal government.

We should mention the Megunticook River that starts at the end of Megunticook Lake and ends by the falls at the Public Landing. Although only three miles long, it was the lifeblood of Camden for many years. It drops 142 feet to sea level, and is the only river in Maine that the ocean

The Conway Boulder was hauled from Chestnut Street and was placed near the Elm Street School.

You are viewing the Megunticook Falls at the end of the river.

Someone looked inside a trolley car.

never enters. There have been as many as ten dams on this little river, but the mills needed only enough stream to turn a water wheel. Today people almost refuse to believe that Camden was a mill town. It was, but the last remaining mill, Knox Woolen Company, died in 1988.

At the Camden Hills State Park there is a convenient road to take you to the top of Mount Battie, with its breathtaking view of Camden, Penobscot Bay and its islands. In the 1930s, there was the CCC camp, and during World War II it was an army barracks. Now it is a great campground.

Coming back to town is the Norumbega, which some call the castle. Mr. Joseph Stearns built it in 1886.

Back in the village, trolley cars began in 1892 and continued for the next thirty-nine years, as the principal mode of transportation for the five coastal communities in Knox County. Some were open cars for good weather and some were closed for winter. Powerhouse Hill in Glen Cove is so called because that is where the power station was located for those electric cars. They had only two serious accidents in those thirty-nine years of operation.

The Boston boat was another mode of transportation. Beyond the condos in Wayfarers Yard was the steamship wharf for the Eastern Steamship Lines. The steamers went from Boston to Bangor, and everyone loved them. It was entertainment for townspeople to watch them arrive and depart. The wharf was sold to the Heilioffs for a lobster holding and packing plant.

That is a brief walking tour of Camden, Maine.

Ten Jewels of Camden

Because I am fortunate enough to have spent a lifetime in "Camden-by-the-Sea," a friend asked me to pick my ten favorite spots. That is a difficult task because there is so much beauty here from which to choose.

High on my list would be Mount Battie, which stands about one thousand feet high. There is a magnificent cyclorama of sweeping woodlands, green meadows, hills and lakes nestled there. The broad expanse of water is beautified by the numerous islands that dot Penobscot Bay from Curtis Island to Bar Harbor. Edna St. Vincent Millay spent much of her time there, which inspired her famous poem "Renascence," which begins,

> *All I could see from where I stood was three long islands and a wood;*
> *I turned and looked the other way and saw three islands in the bay.*

A hotel once had been situated where the tower stands today. A fire raged four days and swept a two-mile path across the summit in 1930, when thousands of people turned out to fight it. A memorial tower to our men who served in World War I has stood as a sentinel since it was dedicated in 1921. The Ku Klux Klan burned a cross there in the early 1930s. There are also fond memories of children who used to climb the mountain for a day's outing and picnics, before the road was built in 1965. Mount Battie holds many more stories.

A similar place of beauty is Mount Megunticook, where the twenty-four-foot cross is a symbol that overlooks Megunticook Lake. The first cross was erected in memory of eleven-year-old Eleanora French, who fell to her death from the cliff in 1864. It has been replaced several times. Thousands of people have made the walk through the woods to see the cross and a spectacular view of the lake.

The Camden Yacht Club was given to the town as a gift.

The Norumbega, for many years a private home, is now one of the finest inns in the United States. Located on upper High Street, it has been a landmark for Camden since Joseph Stearns had it built in 1886, and it is known to many as the "stone castle." Mr. Stearns had traveled the world over, but decided Camden would be the place to live. He had invented the duplex system of telegraphy that made him very wealthy. No description would do the castle justice, as it is so unique.

Just below on the opposite side of High Street is the Whitehall Inn. The owners are very friendly to curious visitors. They are happy to show people the Edna St. Vincent Millay room and wonderful scrapbook about Camden's famous poet. Whitehall Inn maintains the charm and comfort of the early 1900s, with rocking chairs on the porch, checkers and puzzles in the lobby and the quietness of the past.

Cyrus H.K. Curtis had the Camden Yacht Club built in 1911, designed by John Calvin Stevens. It is the only public building in Camden designed by Maine's most noted architect of his day. In September of 1926, Mr. Curtis presented the Camden Yacht Club to the inhabitants of Camden to be used for a yacht club and other community purposes. It is a prime spot, located on the west side of Camden Harbor, overlooking both the inner and outer harbor.

Wayfarer Marine Corporation has to be a favorite of mine. It has been a large part of Camden's economy for many years. It always employed many

The Megunticook Hall was consumed by the Great Fire of Camden.

Curtis Island is one of the jewels in Penobscot Bay.

workers, and probably the largest payroll in Camden during World War II, when fifteen hundred people built ATRs, minesweepers, coal barges and APcs for the war effort. I also think about the 1800s and early 1900s, when such large vessels slid down their ways. That included the second five-masted schooner and the first six-masted schooner ever built. Today it services, repairs and stores yachts from all over the world.

In 1893, after the Great Fire of Camden, the Village Corporation began to lay plans for a building to replace Megunticook Hall. Many residents opposed it, but it is a major attraction in town today. Various shows and entertainers have performed there. During my school years, we all spent our time either in school or at the Camden Opera House. As the floor was flat then, it held the Firemen's Ball, Snow Bowl Carnival Ball, Graduation Ball and Camden High School plays and dances. Changes have been made over the years, but fortunately for Camden residents money came forth for restoration. On July 2, 1994, with research and much labor, a celebration was held to view the lovely Victorian look, exactly as had appeared when it was built over one hundred years ago.

Another favorite has to be the Elm Street School, built in 1869. Untold numbers of Camden residents attended, either as a high school when first built, or grades kindergarten through five for many, many years. It proudly stands as a Camden landmark and is still in use. Many of us have very fond memories of the Elm Street School.

Another place we love, as it serves the whole community, is the Camden Public Library and its surrounding grounds—the Garden Theater (known by many as the amphitheater), designed by Fletcher Steele of Boston, and Camden Shorefront Park (now known as Harbor Park), designed by the Olmsted Brothers. The underground addition to the library, known as the Centennial Wing, had its dedication on September 29, 1996, with the keynote speaker being Barbara Bush. It is a place of beauty for young and old alike.

I immediately thought of nine places and have only one left. It is Curtis Island, a jewel in Penobscot Bay and Camden Harbor. The island was there when Camden's first settler arrived by his small vessel and the African cook aboard claimed it as his island; thus the name Negro Island. On March 12, 1934, the residents of Camden voted to change the name in honor of Curtis H.K. Curtis. He and his daughter, Mary Louise Curtis Bok Zimbalist, beautified Camden in so many ways. The Conovers live there in the summer as caretakers, because people visit this jewel from all over the world.

Some may disagree with my choices, but I defy anyone to choose only ten places in our town of Camden, filled with so much beauty.

About the Author

As a very small child, I felt there could be no better place in which to live than Camden, Maine, so here I have remained. It was most enjoyable growing up in a small town of about thirty-five hundred people, where no one ever locked his door and Camden did not have a police department because it was not needed. The town was one large family where all mothers kept an eye out for every child. It was fine to grow up during the Depression, and because there were no zoning laws most families had a backyard where they grew vegetables, kept a flock of chickens and even a pig or two for food. Wearing hand-me-down clothes was the style, and Christmas was not so commercial, as not many had any money except for necessities.

Classmates were like brothers and sisters because very few families moved into or out of Camden. We were in school every day for thirteen years with the same students. Classes were small, so we all knew each other. World War II had begun the year that I graduated from Camden High School, so I went to work in the shipyard, where they were building vessels for the war effort. The war finally ended but the shipyard continued, and I spent forty-four years there as an accountant and office manager. I supposedly retired twenty years ago, but I have been just as busy serving on committees, the Select Board, lecturing, writing Camden history and teaching adult education. With all the boards I serve on, I can truly say that I have never been bored.

This is the tenth book I have written on "light" Camden history. The first, published in 1984, *Grog Ho! The History of Wooden Shipbuilding in Camden*, was quite by accident. No history had been written on this subject, and while working at the shipyard I realized how important it was to document the industry. That book was followed by *Vintage Views of Camden*, *History of the First Congregational Church in Camden*, *Images of Camden and Rockport*, *Vessel*

Building in Camden, Home Sweet Home, Memories of Camden, More Memories of Camden, Streets Are Paved with Gold and now *Remembering Camden.*

For the past twenty years I have contributed articles to the *Camden Herald*, the *Highlighter*, Villiagesoup.com, *Village Soup Times* and *Discover Maine Magazine.*

One thing led to another, so I also spent twenty years lecturing on Camden history and taught a fifteen-week course in SAD#28 Adult Education called Local History for about eight years.

As I have many unfinished projects at home, I plan to drop my pen and all committees, just as soon as I gain control of my compulsive urge to save Camden history.